How to Build
CHEVY SMALL-BLOCK
CIRCLE-TRACK
RACING ENGINES

JEFF HUNEYCUTT

CarTech®

Edited By: Peter Bodensteiner

ISBN 978-1-61325-009-9

CarTech®

39966 Grand Avenue
North Branch, MN 55056
Telephone (651) 277-1200 • (800) 551-4754 • Fax: (651) 277-1203
www.cartechbooks.com

OVERSEAS DISTRIBUTION BY:

Brooklands Books Ltd.
P.O. Box 146, Cobham, Surrey, KT11 1LG, England
Telephone 01932 865051 • Fax 01932 868803
www.brooklands-books.com

Brooklands Books Aus.
3/37-39 Green Street, Banksmeadow, NSW 2019, Australia
Telephone 2 9695 7055 • Fax 2 9695 7355

Cover:
Keith Dorton of Automotive Specialists built this 600-horsepower small-block Chevy to race in the USAR Pro Cup Series. Chapters 2 through 5 of this book display a variety of Pro Cup parts and engine builds. Dorton's engines have won seven of the past nine Pro Cup championships, and the tricks he uses are applied to just about every other engine he builds.

Title Page:
After decking the heads to achieve the correct combustion chamber volume for the target compression ratio, they are ready to be put in place on the Dirt Late Model engine profiled in Chapter 7.

Back Cover Top:
The Late Model Stock class is one of the most popular in NASCAR's Weekly Racing Series. Because of that, the Late Model Stock engine rules are copied for many other classes by other sanctioning bodies. Learn more about how to build a great engine for this class in Chapter 6.

Back Cover Right:
The no-holds-barred engines found in Dirt Late Model cars are among the most viciously powerful in all of stock car racing. With 800-plus hp, they boast nearly as much peak power as a NASCAR Nextel Cup powerplant, but DLM engines work over a much wider RPM range and, thanks to an aluminum block, also weigh significantly less. Follow the build of one of these incredible engines in Chapter 7 of this book.

Back Cover Left:
The typical entry-level class in stock car racing is called Strictly Stock or Street Stock. These classes almost always mandate stock or stock-style replacement parts. Chapter 5 details a Street Stock-style engine built around the rules you typically see in this class.

TABLE OF CONTENTS

About the Author 4
Acknowledgments 4

Chapter 1: Getting Started 5
Setting Up Shop 5
Tools 7
Measurement Tools 10

Chapter 2: Block Preparation and Machining 13
The Engine 13
Block Choices 15
Identifying Core Shift 17
Installing Freeze Plugs 17
Boring the Cam Tunnel 18
Decking the Block 18
Boring the Cylinders 19
Boring the Lifter Bores 19
Stress Relieving the Block ..20
Final Honing 20
Cleaning 22
Polish the Oil Galleries 22
Final Checks 23

Chapter 3: Short Block Assembly 24
Crankshaft Considerations .24
Connecting Rods 25
Working with Rod/Stroke Ratios 26
Rod Prep 27
Rod Bolt Stretch 29
Pistons 30
Balancing 32
Balance Versus Overbalance 34
Piston Rings 35
Installing the Crank 38
Rod and Piston Assembly ..40

Chapter 4: Cylinder Heads and the Valvetrain 44
Cylinder Head Machine Work 44
Decking 44
Valveguides 45
Spring Seats 46
Screw-In Rocker Studs 46
Valve Seats 46
Valvespring Seat Versus Nose Pressures 47
Adjusting Spring Pressures .48
Valvespring Coil Bind 50
Installing the Cam Bearings 54
Installing the Cam 54
Determining Pushrod Length 54
Camshaft Timing 58
Intake Centerline Method ..60
Finding Piston TDC 60
Measuring Valve Movement 61
Piston-to-Valve Clearance ..62

Chapter 5: Street Stock Engine Build 63
The Block 64
Rotating Assembly 65
Cylinder Heads and Valvetrain 65
Ignition 66
The Spec Sheet 79

Chapter 6: NASCAR Late Model Stock Engine Build 80
The Block 81
Rotating Assembly 81
Cylinder Heads and Valvetrain 81

Oiling 82
The Spec Sheet 97

Chapter 7: Dirt Late Model Engine Build 98
The Block 99
Rotating Assembly 99
Valvetrain 100
Ignition 100
The Spec Sheet 115

Chapter 8: Break-in, Regular Maintenance and Teardown 116
Break-In 116
Regular Maintenance 119
Teardown and Rebuild 122

Engine Build Sheet 127
Source Guide 128

ABOUT THE AUTHOR

Jeff Huneycutt is the senior editor for *Circle Track and Racing Technology* magazine, working primarily in engine technology. He is also a regular contributor to *Stock Car Racing* and *Hot Rod* magazines. His first book, *How to Become a Winning Crew Chief*, co-written with Larry McReynolds, won the Gold Medal from the International Society for Vehicle Preservation for excellence in a technical work. He resides in Charlotte, North Carolina, where he is in daily contact with many of the top engine builders in the stock car racing industry.

ACKNOWLEDGMENTS

This book would not have been possible without the assistance of a host of people. To provide the best and most up-to-date engine-building tips possible, I depended on three of the best engine-building organizations to be found anywhere. Keith Dorton of Automotive Specialists in Concord, North Carolina; Ken and Kevin Troutman of KT Engine Development in Concord, North Carolina; and Tony and Glenn Clements of Clements Racing Engines in Spartanburg, South Carolina. Special thanks also go to Clements' lead engine assembler, Chuck Pridgeon. These gentlemen all carved out significant chunks from their very busy schedules to contribute to this book and also held back no secrets when it came to volunteering information. It is their hard-earned experience and practical knowledge that makes the content of this book something that has never previously been available to the general public. I am extremely grateful to all of you.

I must also thank my editor, Peter Bodensteiner, for his patience and guidance through this project. At several points along the way it felt like the obstacles to getting the best information and getting this book completed were just too great, but Peter always had a solution.

Finally, I would especially like to thank my family—my wife Jennifer and my daughters Meri, Bailey, and Allie. I spent far too many nights in engine shops or behind the computer when I should have been spending it with you. Thank you for your understanding.

GETTING STARTED

Setting Up Shop

Your work area doesn't have to be as nice as this, but to properly build race engines, you will need a clean environment with enough space to work around the engine on a stand comfortably, a large work table or counter top, a place to store your tools, and plenty of light.

A good engine stand is one of the keys to a stress-free engine build. Try to find one that is solidly built instead of saving money on the least expensive stand available, because they aren't as stable. One nice feature is an integrated oil drip pan to keep assembly lube and motor oil off of your floor. If your engine stand doesn't have a drip pan, don't sweat it. They are relatively easy to fabricate, like this one used in engine builder Keith Dorton's shop. Dorton, the owner and lead engine builder of Automotive Specialists, provided lots of information and advice during the writing of this book. He is the most successful engine builder in the history of the USAR Hooters Pro Cup Series and also built the winning engine for the 1990 Daytona 500.

A good air compressor will find a multitude of uses in engine building and other tasks around the shop. Look for one capable of five or six scfm at 90 psi. I prefer this unit from Craftsman. It requires a dedicated 220 outlet, but it's quiet, powerful, and its vertical tank chews up minimal floor space. Be sure to look for a maintenance-free pump, which is definitely a feature you want.

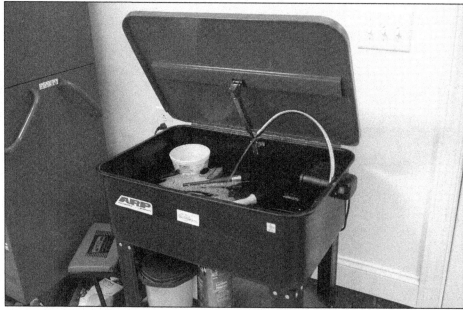

When building a race engine, you will spend almost as much time at the cleaning tank as you will at your assembly bench. This 20-gallon parts washer is a nice compromise between the 50-gallon units most professionals use and the small, 5-gallon tubs. Many newcomers try to save a buck here, but the 5-gallon models are really too small for bigger components like crankshafts.

You will need an engine hoist, or "cherry picker," for handling completed engines. It makes pulling a new block out of the back of your pickup possible if you are trying to manhandle it by yourself. If space is tight, look for one that folds up like this.

Properly cleaning a block as well as many other components requires several brushes of different shapes and sizes. Consider purchasing a set from a supplier such as Powerhouse Products because it is designed as a package specifically for engines. Don't try to get by with the scrub brush you use to wash the dishes.

When planning your engine build, one of the first items to address must be the location where the work will be performed. For most non-professional engine builders, a corner of the garage or workshop winds up as the engine assembly area. This is fine, but if you are going to experience any measure of success, there are a few requirements for you to keep in mind.

The most important thing is that the area is absolutely clean. You cannot be too meticulous in making sure all your engine parts are clean during the assembly process, and this is impossible in a dirty work area. Your assembly area must be separated from dirty work areas to keep contaminants off of your parts. This may sound obvious, but it's a bad idea to try to assemble a race engine in the main area of your racecar shop. There's just too much dust and trash that gets blown around during the day-to-day process of maintaining a racecar. Find an area that you can

clean to your standards and keep it that way.

Be sure your shop area has enough room for you to work comfortably. We're not talking about an aircraft hangar here, but a clear floor space of at least 6x10 feet is the minimum required for an engine assembly stand and for you to comfortably work around it. You will also need a workbench or countertop to work from as well as a place to store your tools and engine components. A solid, smooth floor is nice, as well as a large entrance door for rolling your engines in and out.

Finally, don't forget that you need plenty of good lighting. This may sound more like a luxury than a necessity, but building a quality engine means being able to take accurate measurements and carefully inspect the quality of fit between components. This is difficult to do in poor lighting, and struggling to see is tiring and often leads to mistakes.

It doesn't have to be in your assembly area, but you will need easy

access to a cleaning area and an air compressor. Most engine builders prefer to use a solvent tank for component cleaning, and this is definitely the best option. You can also get away with a workbench, a bucket of solvent, and a few brushes in a pinch. It is important that you do not combine cleaning and assembly on the same workbench.

Access to a compressed air supply will come in handy for everything from blowing water or solvent off of freshly washed components, to operating air tools. Most shops already have an air compressor. If you do, be sure you can reach your assembly area with an air hose. If you don't already own an air compressor, consider purchasing a small 110-volt unit. These are available from many home improvement stores for just a few hundred dollars. They can plug into a standard wall outlet and come in handy for a multitude of jobs—not just engine building. Look for a compressor capable of maintaining five or six scfm at 90 psi.

Tools

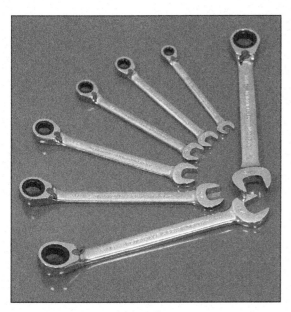

In my opinion, one of the greatest things to happen to hand tools in this decade is the ratcheting box-end wrench. I've upgraded all my combination wrenches to these from Gear Wrench, and they are used much more often than my standard wrenches or ratchets.

Six-point sockets (left) put the most surface area on the head of a fastener, so they can apply more torque without fear of rounding off the edges or otherwise damaging it. Many ultra-strong fasteners used in race engines use a 12-point head that requires a set of 12-point sockets like you see on the right.

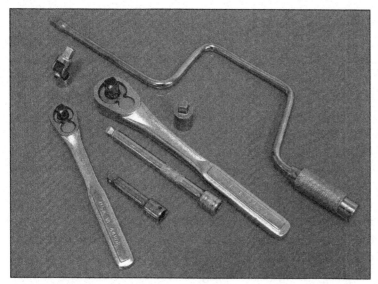

A comprehensive socket set, including a ratchet, extensions, and a universal adaptor that allows you to access hard-to-reach bolts, remains a must-have for every mechanic's tool-box. If you don't already have one, consider adding a speed handle to your tool inventory. It significantly speeds up the pre-fitting process.

You will occasionally need to tap new holes when building race engines. Taps are used even more often to make sure existing holes are clean and free of grit that can throw off a torque reading. I've found that a set of tap sockets (top) attached to a T-handle is much easier to use than a traditional tap chuck (bottom).

A Dremel tool can come in handy for light grinding work, such as de-burring the rough edges created after decking a block. It is also useful for removing casting slag from the oil drain back holes in the valley tray, which will significantly help oil flow in a stock block.

A rod vise is one of those tools you will only find in an engine-builder's shop, but it is the best way to install and remove rod caps without damaging the rods. A dedicated rod vise, like this one from Goodson, mounts in a standard vise and can be easily put away to save space when not in use.

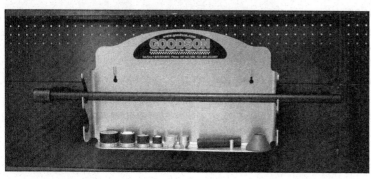

You can have your engine machinist install the cam bearings, but this is a task that really should be done after the entire block has been cleaned thoroughly. A cam bearing installation tool should be the only means for installing the bearings because it ensures that the bearings won't be damaged. It is a bit of an investment but will have paid for itself after your second engine build.

One of the big differences between piston rings for stock rebuilds and those designed for high-performance racing engines is that racing rings require the engine builder to gap them specifically for each cylinder bore. This requires a ring grinder. This hand-powered model from Powerhouse Products is relatively inexpensive and does a good job of keeping the ring ends square.

If you are like me, then the tools you already own are probably worth more than your entire wardrobe. If so, you probably already have almost everything you need to build your own Chevy race engines. If not, don't worry. Very few specialized tools are actually required, and standard hand tools available from any hardware store will work fine.

You will need a complete set of wrenches and sockets in SAE (Society of Automotive Engineers) sizes. This means the wrenches and sockets are sized in fractions of an inch. Unless you are talking about some odd accessories like the alternator pulley nut, there are no metric nuts or bolts on a small-block Chevy 350.

A long-handle set of combination wrenches is invaluable. A combination wrench has a box end on one side and an open end on the other. Make sure your primary wrenches have nice, long handles, which will allow you to generate plenty of torque.

One or two complete sets of SAE sockets should also be considered mandatory. You can get away with only one set, but having a few different styles will really come in handy. Six-point sockets are hexagonal shaped with six angles. These can put the most force on the head of a bolt without damaging it, and so should be used on hex-head nuts and bolts whenever possible.

But some high-end bolts, which are commonly used in race engines, utilize a 12-point head and are not compatible with six-point sockets. For these you must obviously use a set of 12-point sockets. Also, as a general rule, you want to use shorter sockets whenever possible to reduce the chances of a socket slipping off of a bolt and rounding the edges.

Naturally, there are several areas on most motors where a set of deep-well sockets is the only option that will work.

Of course, sockets are useless without ratchets. Ratchets are sorted by the size of the drive stub, which connects to the socket. The most common sizes are 1/4-, 3/8-, and 1/2-inch drives. The most commonly used are 3/8-inch drives, but it is also nice to have a half-inch drive ratchet and companion sockets because the bigger stub size also means the ratchet will have a longer handle. A longer handle makes it easier to put the torque to the bigger nuts and bolts. You don't necessarily have to replicate each socket style in each drive size. If you are just getting started and money is tight, it is better to invest in a few quality sets of 3/8-inch sockets and use a drive adapter to attach those sockets to your 1/2-inch drive ratchet when you need a little more leverage.

One luxury item that is really nice to have when building engines is a speed handle. Over the course of building a complete engine, you will be installing and removing many, many nuts and bolts. Some, like the rod bolts, you will install and remove several times just during the pre-fitting process. Because of this, a speed handle can significantly reduce your build time.

Other tools you will need include screwdrivers (both standard and Phillips head), a dead-blow hammer, pliers, thread taps, a drill, punches, a scribe, and other various tools, depending upon your specific needs. Every engine build is different, so there is no way to tell you every specific tool you will need, but these will cover the majority of your requirements.

Measurement Tools

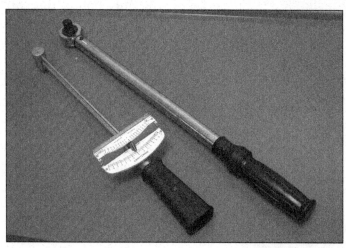

The most-used measurement tool during your build will easily be a torque wrench. Your engine's longevity depends upon properly torqued fasteners, so invest in a good wrench or two (one for small tasks measured in in-lbs, and a larger wrench capable of measuring over 150 ft-lbs).

A feeler gauge costs only a few bucks and is useful for everything from checking valve lash to checking piston clearance in the bore.

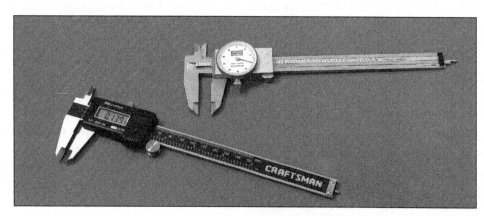

Engine building is all about accuracy, and a dial caliper, while it does the same job as a rule, is infinitely more accurate. Almost every measurement on an engine must be accurate to within plus or minus 0.001 of an inch (or less).

Leave the Plastigage to the stock engine rebuilds. A race engine builder should consider a quality micrometer the only way to measure such things as rod and main journal sizes.

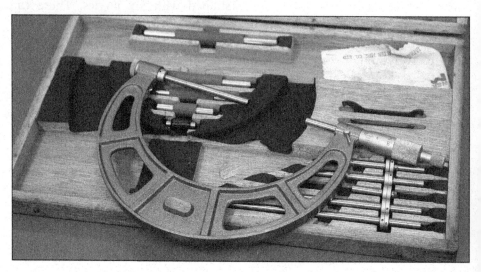

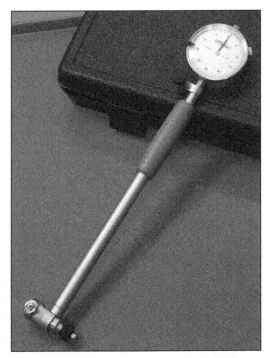

A CC kit is yet another one of those tools owned only by a race-engine builder. It may be tough to spend the money on one because it serves only a single purpose, but it's also the only way to reliably measure the volume of the combustion chambers on your cylinder heads as well as cylinder volume when the piston is at TDC (Top Dead Center). Without this information you cannot accurately compute the completed engine's compression ratio. Making a mistake here is a quick way to be declared illegal.

When used in conjunction with a micrometer, a dial bore gauge is the quickest and most accurate tool for measuring bearing clearances for the rods, mains, and cam. It is also useful for checking cylinder bores and other areas.

A dial indicator on an adjustable stand can be used to measure everything from piston TDC, to camshaft endplay, to movement of the rocker stud, as shown here. The indicator gauge should be able to measure to at least 0.001 inch. There are gauges capable of 0.0001-inch increments; they are expensive but will improve your precision.

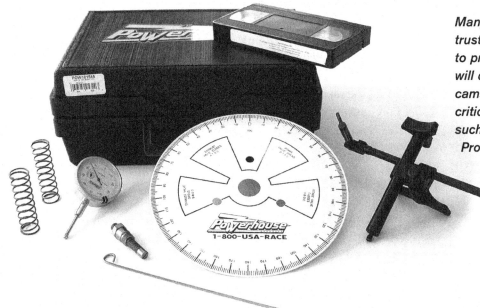

Many engine builders begin by simply trusting their camshaft manufacturer to provide the correct cam. But most will quickly begin degreeing in their camshafts, since cam timing is so critical to maximizing power. A kit such as this one from Powerhouse Products makes degreeing your cams simple and painless.

A well-manufactured and properly installed connecting rod rarely fails in a race engine. Proper installation, however, requires that you measure rod bolt stretch and not just depend on a torque reading. This is because bolts torqued to the same number will have varying degrees of stretch when used with different lubricants. Ideally, most rod bolts should be installed with 0.005 to 0.006 of an inch of stretch. The only way to measure this is with a stretch gauge, like this one from ARP (Automotive Racing Products).

A race motor capable of good power and durability is not only a product of the components you put into it, but also of how well it is put together. Without the correct tools, it is impossible to quantify such things as how tightly the bolts hold the rod and main caps together; how much clearance there is between the rod, main, and cam journals and the bearings; and even the engine's compression ratio. For these tasks and more you must have and be able to appropriately use the correct measurement tools. Many of these are fairly common in general automotive applications, but a few are quite specific to building race engines.

The one measurement tool that is absolutely necessary is a torque wrench. A torque wrench lets you specify exactly how much twisting force is applied to a fastener. Too little torque on a bolt does not provide enough clamping force, while too much torque can cause it to fail. Nearly every bolt inside the engine should be tightened with a torque wrench because every component in a race engine walks that thin line between ultimate performance and failure.

There are several different styles of torque wrenches, but no matter which style you choose, make sure you purchase a quality unit. Your engine's health depends upon the wrench's ability to measure torque accurately.

Other measurement tools that you should consider "must-haves" include a feeler gauge and a pair of dial calipers. A feeler gauge is useful for determining such things as ring gap, valve lash, and even crankshaft endplay. Dial calipers, either analog or digital, are much more accurate than trying to read a ruler or a tape measure. In general, all measurements must be accurate to within less than 0.001 of an inch, and this is only possible with quality measuring instruments.

The next step in engine-building accuracy is to purchase a dial bore gauge and a set of micrometers. The micrometer is extremely useful for measuring the diameter of a round surface. A dial bore gauge is useful for determining the diameter of a cylinder. A dial bore gauge can help you determine the quality of the honing job your machinist did on your cylinders or whether the connecting rods you wish to re-use after a rebuild have been damaged by detonation. Together, the micrometer and dial bore gauge are used to determine bearing clearances for your rod and main journals.

A dial indicator mounted on an adjustable stand, preferably with a magnetic base, also comes in very handy. The magnetic base allows you to position it just about anywhere on a cast-iron block, and you can use it to check such things as crankshaft and camshaft endplay, piston TDC, and even rocker arm movement, among other things. A dial indicator accurate to within 0.001 of an inch can be had relatively inexpensively from most tool distributors. You can also easily measure rod bolt stretch with a dial indicator mounted on a special fixture. You can begin by doing without these tools or borrowing from a friend. By the time you begin the build for your second engine, however, you will be ready for a set of your own.

Finally, there are other measurement tools that are necessary only to race-engine builders. A perfect example is when the rulebook mandates a minimum combustion chamber size for the cylinder heads or a maximum compression ratio. To produce as much power as possible, you will need to make sure your engine pushes these limits without exceeding them. If you are just getting started you can trust your cylinder head manufacturer's chamber volume specification to calculate compression ratio, but eventually you will want to measure this yourself.

A CC test kit uses a graduated burette that measures how much liquid an area, such as a combustion chamber, will hold. This allows you to measure your combustion chamber volume so accurately that you can even account for how deeply the spark plug intrudes into the chamber. Armed with this knowledge, you can calculate your compression ratio accurately to the tenth. You can then be sure all your hard work won't get thrown out after failing inspection in the tech shed.

BLOCK PREPARATION
AND MACHINING

There is no magic involved in building great race motors. It's not voodoo, and there really is very little mystery in building race-winning Chevrolet motors. What is required is the temperament of a perfectionist (I won't call it anal, but it doesn't hurt), an obsession with cleanliness, a modicum of organization, and a willingness to learn. Oh, and a handful of specialized tools, but that's the easiest part. The goal of this book is to help you, at least a little bit, with all of those things.

The Engine

When it comes to stock car racing, in any class from Street Stock to NASCAR Nextel Cup, no engine package has enjoyed the success of Chevrolet's venerable small block. Because of its success and popularity, it enjoys a broad base of support from both General Motors and aftermarket manufacturers. Performance parts for the small block are abundant, and because of competition from many different manufacturers, the cost of building a Chevy race

No matter how well you assemble your race engine, you cannot overcome the hurdles created by a poorly prepared engine block. Find an engine machine shop capable of properly machining your block so that you will have the perfect foundation for your race engine.

motor is generally less than for any other brand.

The Chevy small block was first introduced in 1955 and remains in production today in the form of the LS-series motors. For the purposes of stock car racing, we are concerning ourselves only with the 350-ci design, produced from 1968 until 1996. These engines used a 4.00-inch bore with a 3.500-inch stroke. In 1968, General Motors increased the main journal size to 2.45 inches, and the rod journal size was standardized at 2.100 inches. These are commonly referred to as "large journal" blocks. The connecting rod length remained at 5.7 inches. Though stock car race motors can be constructed from the 305- and 400-inch motor designs, they are rare, so I won't discuss them in this book.

There are a few additional variations among the 350-ci engines over the years. In 1986, Chevrolet replaced the two-piece rear main seal design with a one-piece seal in order to reduce oil leaks and subsequent warranty repairs. The one-piece rear main seal design required changes to both the block and the crank, as well as minor changes to the oil pan, but none of the changes affect power output.

The one-piece design has never really taken hold in racing circles because almost all performance cranks are manufactured for use with two-piece rear main seals. Stock two-piece rear main blocks, however, are becoming more difficult to find. Thankfully, it is relatively easy to convert a block from a one-piece rear main seal design to the older two-piece in order to work with many aftermarket performance crankshafts. No major machining operations must be performed on the block, but it may require drilling and tapping a couple of holes. In addition to the adapter plate, performing this conversion also requires a small fixture to simulate crankshaft location.

Another important feature for race engine builders is the four-bolt main block, introduced in 1968. It was used mainly in trucks and a few high-performance applications. Most

people refer to it simply as a "truck block." Other than the four-bolt mains, there are no other differences, meaning that the crankshafts are interchangeable. A four-bolt block is preferable over a block with two-bolt mains because the extra bolts add rigidity to the main caps as well as the structure of the block itself. In lower-horsepower Street Stock racing classes, an engine with two-bolt mains generally should not be a problem. If you are racing in high-horsepower classes, however, it is relatively easy for your machine shop to upgrade a two-bolt block to one that will accept four-bolt main caps.

No matter how well you assemble your race engine, you cannot overcome the hurdles created by a poorly prepared engine block. Find an engine machine shop capable of properly machining your block so that you will have the perfect foundation for your race engine.

The analogy that the machine work performed on a block before a build is like laying a solid foundation for a new house has been overused for years. It's a tired comparison that I hesitate to mention except for the fact that it's very true. It doesn't matter how much thought you put into parts selection or how much effort you dedicate to assembly—it's all wasted time if the block isn't cast

The rear main seal was re-designed in 1986 to reduce oil seepage. The seal was changed from a two-piece design to a one-piece seal. This change also affected the block and crank. The one-piece design isn't bad, but it is much easier to find aftermarket performance cranks designed to work with the two-piece seal. Fortunately, it is relatively easy to add an adaptor that accepts the two-piece seal to your one-piece style block.

A stock factory block with four-bolt main caps and a two-piece rear seal is a rare sight. This block was ordered new from GM Performance Parts (GMPP) for a Street Stock engine build. They are no longer available new, but good cores are still out there.

correctly and machined within the proper tolerances.

A quality block is critical because it houses and serves as the attachment point for every other engine component. Likewise, every moving part is designed to work best in a precise location relative to one or more of the block's three most critical reference centerlines: The crankshaft centerline, the camshaft centerline, and each of the eight cylinder bore centerlines.

Of course, this doesn't mean that you must have a PhD in geometry to build race engines, but you must understand how one part of the engine can affect many other areas in ways you may not expect. For example, if the camshaft centerline is in the wrong position, the lifter bores won't allow the lifters to contact the cam lobes correctly, which can lead to a destroyed cam.

Because the purpose of this book is to help you build your own Chevrolet racing engines, the working assumption is that you will perform as many of the steps as you possibly can. The one area where most racers have to hand off the work is the machining that must be performed on the block and cylinder heads as well as the crankshaft, rods, and other parts of the engine. This is because the machinery required to perform these processes is very specialized and quite expensive. This equipment also requires a great deal of expertise to operate properly. Unless you are already building engines for a living, or have a best friend who does, it's really a much better idea to hire a machine shop for this work.

The first step is to find an engine machine shop capable of doing the machine work you need and doing it well. If you don't already have a good working relationship with an engine builder, the best place to gather good recommendations is the racetrack. Nobody has more experience with racing engines and engine builders than racers. If you aren't already racing, visit a local track or two and ask around. Most racers will

be more than happy to help anyone who is looking to go racing.

While you are gathering information, your main question should be "Who does good machine work?" But you can also use the opportunity to find out more. You may also wish to ask about prices, if the machinist is easy to deal with and if he normally turns around work in the time promised. After all, the best machine work in the world won't do you much good if you can't get it back in time to build your engine and make the race. When you do find a machinist you want to work with, don't be afraid to discuss exactly what machining operations he recommends for your engine and the reason why each operation is necessary.

Finally, before hiring out work, you should be aware that most race-engine builders only guarantee complete engines will crank and make it to the first turn. If they are providing the machine work and you are completing the assembly, no one will even guarantee that much.

Before beginning assembly you should be able to check the work with your own measurements. We'll show you how to do that in future chapters so that you can spot machining problems before the engine is assembled, and before it's too late.

Block Choices

The first step is to select your engine block. If you race in more restrictive classes or in a spec engine class, you likely are very limited in which engine blocks you can use. If

A Chevy Bow Tie block has several advantages over the stock block it is based upon, though it can be hard to tell the difference from a quick glance because both maintain the same critical dimensions. First, the Bow Tie block is manufactured under tighter tolerances, meaning core shift is less of an issue. Four-bolt mains come standard, and there is extra material in highly stressed areas. This makes the Bow Tie block heavier, but it is better able to withstand the stresses of high-horsepower engine packages.

If your rules allow, a block utilizing four-bolt main caps is almost always preferable in racing applications. This is because they provide a more stable foundation for the spinning crankshaft, and by extension, the rest of the rotating assembly. Splayed caps (where the outside bolts thread into the block on an angle) are also preferable because they help stabilize the entire block.

Engine blocks with the two-piece rear main seal are an older design but generally preferred by engine builders because most aftermarket crankshafts are built for the two-piece seal design.

the rulebook is more forgiving, you have a few options available. In entry-level racing classes with lower-power engines, the basic choice is a stock block. Chevy's first-generation V-8 was produced in massive quantities between 1968 and '96 and they are still relatively easy to find. You can purchase a stock 350 block as a used junkyard core or new from GM Goodwrench.

Stock blocks are available in a few variations. The most important difference is that you can find blocks with either two- or four-bolt main bearing caps. They generally cost a little more, but if you can afford it, a block with four-bolt mains is definitely the way to go. The two extra bolts help hold the caps more securely and provide stability for the crank and bearings, which becomes critical as the horsepower increases.

You should be aware that General Motors made a relatively significant alteration to the engine block in 1986 when it changed the rear main seal from a two-piece design to a single-piece style. This change was made to reduce oil seepage from the back of the block. The one-piece seal required changes to the block and crank, among other things. Most racers prefer the two-piece design because it eases disassembly for rebuilds and, more importantly, most high-performance cranks available are built for that style engine. If you have a newer block, adapters for the two-piece seal are readily available.

In higher-horsepower applications, a thin-walled stock block becomes a liability. If your rules allow it and you are exceeding 500 horsepower, you will want to consider a block based on the classic Chevy small-block parameters but constructed with racing in mind.

Pro Tip: Go Light

Although it may sound odd at first, Keith Dorton says in the right situation, a stock block is faster than an equivalent engine built using a Bow Tie or other aftermarket block. Because they are designed to be stronger, race blocks can be 40 to 60 pounds heavier than a stock Chevy block.

In restricted-power racing classes where a stock block can handle the stress, this weight reduction is significant. Even though the car may have to meet a minimum weight (usually 3,200 pounds), that weight savings from the block can be transferred to lead positioned in the frame rails. So even though it may not relate directly to horsepower, a good engine builder still has to consider all of the factors that affect the performance of the racecar, including handling.

Chevrolet labels their high-performance pieces "Bow Tie" blocks, but aftermarket race blocks are available from other manufacturers as well.

Companies such as Dart and World Products have been producing their own Chevy-based block and cylinder head castings for years and boast fantastic quality. The differences between a stock block and a race block are normally tighter tolerances for machining and core shift, thicker cylinder walls, improved oil and water passages, and reinforced areas to address traditional weak spots in the stock block. They are also available in either cast iron or aluminum with iron cylinder sleeves.

The aftermarket race blocks also have additional features to differentiate them from Bow Tie blocks. For example, the sides of World Products' Chevy block are "bulged" out at each of the cylinders. This was done to allow even larger bore diameters and still provide an adequate water jacket for sufficient cooling. Some blocks are also designed to allow stroker cranks without the need for grinding for clearance on the interior of the block. The block that best suits your needs will largely be determined by the engine's estimated power, your rulebook, and your budget.

Identifying Core Shift

Core shift is a by-product of the casting process and is most common in older, mass-produced blocks. When blocks are cast, there is the possibility that the two sides of the mold aren't lined up perfectly. This becomes more of a problem as the molds become older because the locating dowel pins can wear, allowing misalignment of the two halves. In low-volume Bow Tie or aftermarket high-performance blocks, this is rarely a problem.

If the camshaft housing bore isn't centered in the cam boss on the front of the block, it doesn't necessarily mean that the block is junk. But it does mean that further measurements should be made before using the block. Engine builders like Automotive Specialists have instruments that can be used to measure water jacket thickness throughout the block to make sure that core shift hasn't weakened it in a critical area. A sonic tester will also help you determine whether the cylinder walls have been made too thin as a result of core shift.

Installing Freeze Plugs

Racing engines endure extreme vibration and stress that an over-the-road engine will never be subjected to. Because of that, it's a good idea to

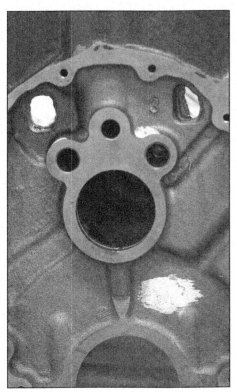

The easiest way to spot an engine block affected by core shift is to examine the cam housing bore on the front of the block. If the cam bore is off-center in the cam boss that could be a sign of core shift, which will require further attention.

Pro Tip: Checking Cam-to-Crank Orientation

After a thorough visual inspection, one of the first measurement steps taken at Automotive Specialists is to check the cam-to-crank centerline distance. Automotive Specialists uses a fabricated measurement fixture, but other methods are available on the market. Machinist Earl Mark says that most Chevy blocks are correct in the cam-to-crank centerlines, but approximately 40 percent require some adjustment. The cam bore housing in Bow Tie blocks are shipped undersized, so any misalignment can be corrected when the cam bores are opened up.

Checking the distance between the cam and crank centerlines isn't a process that most engine machine shops normally perform, but it can correct valvetrain geometry problems that might plague you later on.

Boring the Cam Tunnel

Most Bow Tie blocks ship with the cam bore housings under- sized so that they can be bored and honed to the correct size and in the correct location by the engine block machinist. The Bow Tie bores are 2.00 inches and need to be opened up to 2.282 inches (50 mm) to accept roller cam bearings. If Automotive Specialists is building a non-roller bearing engine, the cam bores will be opened up to 2.120 inches. This procedure also allows for adjustments to be made if the cam-to-crank centerline distance isn't correct from the foundry. The larger camshaft housing bore is an advantage because it allows a cam with a larger base circle, which increases the camshaft's overall rigidity. With the high spring pressures used in today's engines, this is becoming increasingly important.

The cam tunnel will be bored to within 0.002 to 0.0025 inches of the final size and then honed the rest of the way.

Decking the Block

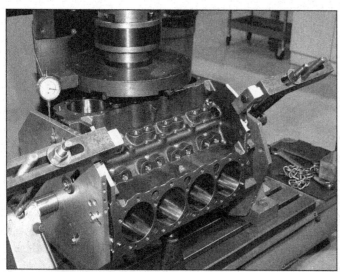

After the cam bores are complete, the block is placed in a BHJ fixture that locates the crank centerline and allows the block to be decked 90 degrees. The deck of the block should always be surfaced before a build. If the block is new, cutting the deck is necessary to get the correct compression ratio. If the engine has already been run and is being rebuilt, repeated heat cycles can cause the deck of the block to warp. The deck surface must be cleaned up on a decking machine to promote a good seal with the head gasket. Ideally, the plane of the deck should be perpendicular with the crank centerline and within 0.0005 inches of perfectly flat in all directions. The surface finish this operation produces on the deck is important as it ensures proper sealing with the head gasket, especially around the water passages.

Here, the distance from the face of the deck to the crank centerline is being measured. When maximizing compression ratio is critical, you may want to wait to final-deck the block until after you are able to mock up the engine and measure the distance from the top of the piston at TDC to the deck.

Boring the Cylinders

Another fixture is added to the BHJ that locates the cylinder bore centers. Bow Tie blocks ship with undersized bores of approximately 3.980 inches. This ensures that there is plenty of material to true up the bores when they are cut to the standard 4.00-inch size (or larger). Stock blocks often do not have cylinder walls with enough material to allow this. If you are using a stock block, especially on a rebuild, you may have to determine if there is any cylinder bore misalignment and whether it is repairable. If it isn't, you will have to determine if it is something you are willing to live with, or if the better course of action is to discard the block and start over.

Boring the Lifter Bores

This fixture ensures that each of the lifter bores is perfectly centered over its corresponding cam lobe. If they aren't perfectly centered you can have the bores opened up and insert a sleeve to correct lifter alignment. You also want to employ the biggest lifters you can use, because larger-diameter lifters allow for more aggressive cam lobe profiles. If the rules allow, have the lifter bores opened up to 0.875 inches.

pin the freeze plugs in place so you know they won't blow out at an inopportune time and spill coolant all over the track. When this happens, your back tires will likely roll right though it, which often leads to a spin and wreck. Plus, it's a relatively simple procedure.

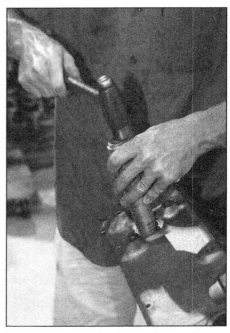

Install the freeze plugs as you normally would with a hammer and punch. New plugs should be used with each rebuild. If you wish, you can use a little green Loctite around the edges of each plug to ensure a good seal.

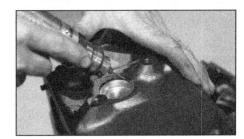

Drill three holes just above the lip of each plug (on the chamfer of the plug bore in the block) at a 45-degree angle using a #38 bit. Each hole should be approximately 0.300 inches deep. Be careful not to go deeper or you might drill into the water jacket.

Some builders prefer to tap the holes and use button-head screws, but there are freeze-plug pins made specifically for this purpose. These work well and save you the step of having to tap the holes. Simply put a drop of green Loctite on each pin and tap them into place.

Stress Relieving the Block

For years, many racers preferred to race blocks that had already seen use on the road. This is because the repeated heat cycles stress relieved or "settled" the material in the blocks and made them more stable. Shot-peening the metal does the same thing to an extent, but today there are even better methods to stress-relieve a new block.

Automotive Specialists uses a Meta-Lax machine on all new blocks before performing the final honing processes. A Meta-Lax machine is actually a vibratory table. The block is bolted in place and left to vibrate for a few minutes. It may not seem like much, but it does help settle new blocks so that the critical dimensions will remain stable after several races. A block can also be

A vibratory table such as this can help align the molecules in a block and help make it more stable.

thermally stress relieved by essentially baking it, but this must be done before any machining processes have taken place.

Final Honing

Proper honing leaves a crosshatch pattern of tiny grooves in the cylinder bore. These grooves are important because they allow a thin film of oil to remain on the cylinder walls after the rings have moved past. This improves cylinder sealing as well as ring and cylinder bore life. The trick is getting the correct texture in the crosshatch to suit the rings you plan to use; too deep or too shallow and you will compromise both engine power and life.

Keith Dorton recommends leaving the bores 0.005 inches undersized

Using the proper measurement tools is critical in the final honing steps because it is here you are ensuring that the final tolerances are met. In modern race engines, oil control is improved by keeping very tight tolerances, but this means even the slightest mistake can lead to a spun bearing. A quality machinist will check and re-check his bore sizes several times during the honing process to make sure he doesn't overshoot the mark.

During the line-honing stage, Dorton recommends rotating the block at least once to help maintain the consistency of the bore from the front to the back of the block.

The bores are honed in at least two steps (often three) with progressively finer stones until the perfect bore diameter with the perfect crosshatch pattern is achieved. Check with your ring manufacturer for their recommendations for the final stone to get the best crosshatch finish for your chosen rings.

after the boring process, and removing the remaining material by honing. At least three honing steps will be used to bring the bore to final diameter. Each step will use progressively finer stones so that the crosshatch will be perfect just as the cylinder reaches the correct size.

Dorton starts with a 525 or 518 stone and hones the cylinders until they are 0.003 inches undersized. Next, he moves to a 625 stone until it is 0.001 inches under. The last thousandth is finished up with an 820 stone. You cannot start with an 820 stone because it would take all day to cut the excess metal and would generate too much heat in the process. Finally, Dorton says he finishes off each cylinder with a cork-type stone, which works well with most types of rings.

Currently, engine builders for professional racing teams are experimenting with different honing processes, which may improve the process even further. Some, like diamond honing or hot honing (which heats the engine block before honing to simulate the expansion of a running engine) show promising

Make sure your machinist uses a torque plate when performing the final hone on the cylinders. This simulates the forces placed on a block when the heads are torqued in place. Also, an old head gasket that's the same as the one you plan to use on the final build should always be used between the torque plate and the block. The head bolts should be torqued to the same specs that will be used to hold the cylinder heads in place.

A good crosshatch pattern is also necessary in the lifter bores, so they must be honed, too.

results, but these processes are still too expensive to be common among hobby level racers.

Cleaning

The importance of cleanliness when building a race engine cannot be overstressed. You will be cleaning the block again once you receive it from the machine shop, but a good

When it comes to cleaning your block, you are constrained to a water hose and soap. Have the engine machinist run your block through his hot tank, which often uses a mild chemical solution to help cut the grease. Be aware that this doesn't get the oil galleries clean. These areas will still need special attention.

Polish the Oil Galleries

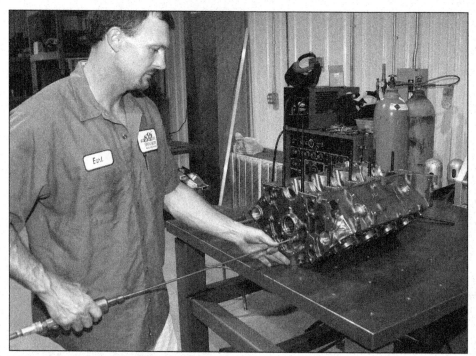

Any contamination left inside the oil galleries will head straight to a bearing surface or the valvetrain as soon as you crank the engine, so it is critical that all galleries are thoroughly cleaned. The easiest way to do this is with a long, 1/4-inch-diameter rod chucked in a drill or die grinder. Notch one end of the rod so that you can slide a strip of emery cloth through it. Use the strip of emery cloth as a flapper to clean and polish all of the oil galleries.

Pro Tip:
Lubricate the Cam Thrust Bearing

To increase lubrication to the cam thrust bearing, cut a small notch in the front of the first cam housing bore. You can do this with a hand file. This will allow just enough oil to leak by to lubricate the cam thrust bearing.

Sonic testing is a good, non-invasive way to determine the thickness of surfaces, such as cylinder walls, where you can only see one side (in the case of cylinder walls the back side is inaccessible because of the water jacket).

session in a hot tank goes a long way toward getting all the accumulated crud and metal shavings out of the block.

Final Checks

Before the block is ready to be taken back to your shop, you need to ensure that two more tests are performed. All the machining processes that have taken place on the block can sometimes reveal casting flaws or thin areas. It may have already been done, but have the cylinder walls sonic tested again to make sure the boring and honing work hasn't created thin spots. Likewise, now is the perfect time to have the water jackets pressure tested to verify that they will hold water.

Because it isn't practical to sonic test every inch of surface area in the block, you should always have the block pressure checked after all the machining processes are complete. This will ensure that a casting flaw hasn't been uncovered during the machining operations. Such a leak will allow coolant into areas where it doesn't belong.

SHORT BLOCK ASSEMBLY

Preparing the block is a long and sometimes tedious process. Once all the checking and machining processes are finished and the block has been completely cleaned of any debris, grease, and other contaminants, you are ready to begin building your short block.

Of course, the process of measuring, pre-fitting, and cleaning has only just begun. As mentioned earlier, actual engine assembly is only a small portion of the process of quality engine building. Now that the block is correct, you will also need to ensure that each component that goes into it is correct as well. The best place to begin is with the crankshaft.

Crankshaft Considerations

As you advance to higher-level classes, rules generally become less restrictive about what crank designs you can use. A stock crank has very limited usefulness in racing, especially if it is cast iron. Generally, you will only want to use a stock crank in classes with cheap claimer rules that prevent you from spending any real

By utilizing such tricks as pendulum-cut counterweights, it is possible to significantly lighten a forged steel crankshaft. A forged crank can be as light as 44 pounds while still being able to handle upwards of 500 hp. This technology, however, does not come without a price.

Most racing cranks use a wide fillet to increase strength. A fillet radius of 0.125 inch will work well for most applications.

money on the engine build. The problem isn't only increased horsepower, but the shock a grippy racing tire can impart upon the crank can cause problems as well. Every time the driver brakes to slow the car

through the corners, the driveline creates significant tension on the crank. Also, a shock is sent through the driveline and forward to the crank each time the tires break and then regain traction.

There are several factors to consider in a quality racing crank. Almost all performance cranks are forged and hardened from 4340 steel. Ideally, a crank needs to be very stiff in order to resist flex caused by eight connecting rods pushing and pulling along its length (which can wipe out bearings if the crank is too flexible). The crank should not be so stiff that it becomes brittle and cracks or shatters.

Most lower-cost racing cranks hover around 50 pounds because that's the lightest many rulebooks allow. A 50-lb crank can be forged without many lightening measures. Lightening holes cut only in the rod journals leave plenty of material in critical areas, meaning the crank will be quite strong. A crank can be lightened further by undercutting the counter-weights and gun-drilling some of the main journals. Somewhere around 44 to 45 pounds is the limit for a lightweight crank that will stand up to oval-track abuse. Billet cranks are also available, but they are very expensive and usually the choice of drag racers with engines capable of well over 1,000 hp.

A good way to free up some power is by reducing the size of the rod journals. This is done to lower bearing speed, which reduces friction. The more RPMs the engine turns, the greater the power savings. The standard Chevy rod journal size is 2.100 inches, but popular sizes for racing are also 2.00 and 1.889 inches. The 1.889 size is commonly referred to as a "Honda journal" because this is the stock size for Honda four-cylinder engines.

Be aware that running Honda journals can cut the useful lifespan of a crankshaft because the smaller journal size reduces the amount of over-

lap area between the rod journals and main journals. This arrangement also requires a specially designed crank to make the oil passages work correctly. It can be costly, but in many cases it's a worthwhile investment.

In contrast to the rod journals, many engine builders prefer cranks with the larger main journals. Standard main journal size for the 350 is 2.45 inches. The Chevy Bow Tie block is available with both the "350 Main" size and the "400 Main," which is 2.65 inches. You can even find aftermarket blocks with undersized 2.30-inch mains. A smaller main journal also helps reduce bearing speed, but the loss of overall strength is often not worth it.

Connecting Rods

A decade ago, a connecting rod failure was a common problem in racing. Today, these components are so well designed and manufactured that you rarely hear of a true rod failure. Quality racing rods have become so affordable that there is no reason to run a stock rod unless your rules require it.

The trick is to use the lightest rod that will withstand your projected

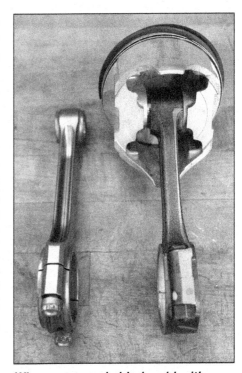

When compared side-by-side, it's easy to see the differences between a stock rod (right) and a purpose-built racing rod, such as this one from Carrillo. The I-beam style stock rod is constructed from powdered metal while the H-beam race piece is forged. The forged rod saves weight by eliminating balance pads and increases strength by utilizing high-quality cap-screw bolts instead of the stocker's through bolts, which are secured by nuts.

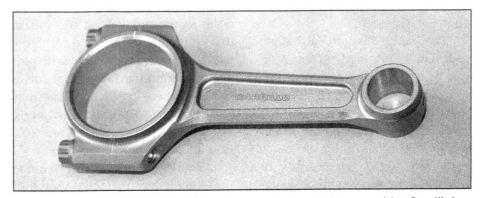

If you are racing in a limited power class, you may want to consider Carrillo's A-beam rod. It is a variation on the I-beam where much of the flanges are cut away. Besides being light, it requires fewer machining processes to manufacture, which makes it less expensive.

They may cost a little more, but connecting rods with bronze bushings in the pin end will help reduce the chances of a wristpin galling in the rod if the oil pressure drops for any reason. To further guard against pin galling, you should chamfer the oil hole in the pin end of the rod. Do this on both the bushing side and the rod exterior.

HP. Powdered metal rods designed for sportsman-level performance applications are relatively new on the scene and boast surprisingly low prices for the budget-minded engine builder. Howards Racing Components is one company leading the charge in this area.

For more strength, use forged rods. On a very high-end build, you can go with a fully machined forged rod. This is a rod forged with extra material that is then cut away to the rod's final dimensions in a CNC machine. This machining process cuts away any surface irregularities that can cause weaknesses in a standard forging. Regular forged rods, however, are so advanced that this is only necessary if you are pushing the absolute limits of your engine package.

Most rod designs fall into one of two categories, I-beams or H-beams. I-beam rods are the classic design you see with stock rods. A newer off-shoot of that design is Carrillo's A-beam connecting rod, which is essentially a narrowed I-beam. It is very light and since it requires fewer machining processes, it is also relatively inexpensive. A-beams are a great candidate for low- to mid-level engines of up to 450 to 500 hp. H-beam rods are much more resistant to the twisting forces exerted upon them and, when manufactured correctly, are a stronger design.

The aftermarket selection of Chevy rods is practically endless, but most circle track builders stick with a few proven standards. The best rod lengths for small blocks vary, from the stock length of 5.700 inches to 6.00 inches and slightly longer. Bushed pin ends are popular to help prevent galling, and cap-screw fasteners, which thread into the body of the rod and eliminate the nut, are also widely accepted.

One trend that has fallen by the wayside in terms of popularity is the pin-oiling rod. This design uses a small oiling hole cut through the beam of the rod to provide pressurized oil to the wristpin. This was done to prevent galling the pin in dry sump engines. Using a combination of thicker, less flexible wristpins and diamond-hard coatings solves most of these problems. You may still be able to find pin-oiling rods, but they are usually a band-aid solution for bigger problems.

Finally, it's often quite easy to find a good deal on a set of used rods from touring race teams or a high-end race engine builder. Teams racing for big money will often discard a set of otherwise good rods after a

certain number of engine cycles rather than risk a failure. These are usually high-quality pieces and many engine builders have benefited from getting these rods at a fraction of their original cost.

Do be very careful when exploring this route. You need to know as much as possible about the pieces you are considering. How many races (or laps) did these rods run? Was there any type of engine failure when these rods were in the engine? If the engine was run hot or experienced detonation, the rods can be slightly damaged in ways that are difficult to detect. At the very least, each rod should be Magnafluxed before installing them into your engine.

If you are a veteran of building stock motors, you will be glad to know that the age-old task of lightening and balancing a set of rods is essentially no longer necessary. Dorton says that almost all race rods arrive balanced to within a gram. If he comes across a set that isn't balanced to his liking he simply sends them back. Grinding on a purpose-built race rod isn't wise, since they do not have balance pads on each end like a stock rod. A race rod is designed to be as light as possible and has zero extra material that can be ground away. Don't even risk it.

Working with Rod/Stroke Ratios

The rod/stroke ratio is simply the length of the connecting rod (from center to center) divided by the stroke. For example, a stock 350 Chevrolet with a 5.7-inch rod and a 3.5-inch stroke has a rod/stroke ratio of 1.629. Many race motors squeeze a 6.0-inch rod into the same package, bumping the ratio up to 1.714.

The longer ratio creates more "dwell time," or a greater percentage of time the piston stays near TDC. This can be an advantage because more cylinder pressure is created by the extended piston dwell time, once the spark plug ignites the mixture.

Using the longest connecting rod possible also has a secondary advantage: By increasing the rod length, you can raise the pin height and reduce the piston's compression height. The compression height is the distance between the center of the pin and the piston face. Although the piston is aluminum and the connecting rod is steel, lengthening the rod in order to reduce the compression distance will almost always reduce overall reciprocating weight by allowing a smaller, lighter piston.

Many engine builders believe a large rod/stroke ratio is helpful because it reduces piston side loading on the cylinder walls, but Dorton says this really isn't much of an issue for stock car racing. There are limits, however, to how much rod/stroke ratio you want. If you increase the ratio too much, you can create so much dwell time that detonation becomes a problem. Combining increased dwell time with a very aggressive, high-lift cam can also create piston-to-valve clearance issues. The key is to find the best piston available with the shortest compression distance and then match it with a connecting rod that gets you the proper deck height.

Rod Prep

Excellent attention to detail is critical when it comes to preparing your rods for installation in the engine. Achieving the correct amount of clearance between the bearings and the crank's rod journals is critical to maximizing the life and performance of your engine. The same holds true for the pin end of the rod.

The popular rule of thumb when it comes to finding the correct bearing clearance is 0.001 of an inch between the bearing and the crank journal for every inch of journal diameter. Given that a small journal Chevy small-block is 2.00 inches, and the popular Honda journal size is just 1.889 inches, clearances between the crank journal and the rod bearings are incredibly tight. Dorton likes to hold the clearance between 0.0018 and 0.0022 inches.

The difficulty isn't accurately measuring to such levels of precision, but knowing exactly where to measure. Most cranks, no matter the manufacturer, tend to have predictable variances in the crank journals. Even on a high-end crank, you can see as much as 0.0002 inches more thickness in the diameter of the journal at the oiling holes. This extra material doesn't extend all the way around the journal; it is only at the oiling holes. So as long as the "bump" measures 0.0002 inches or less, the crank is acceptable.

Also, most crank journals will be thicker at both ends (at the beginning of the fillet radius), get thinner, and then thicken up again in the middle. Again, I am only talking about a couple tenths of one one-thousandth of an inch, but if you are trying to hold your tolerances to plus or minus 0.001, it is something you should be aware of. When measuring journal size, find the largest diameter, which is usually in the middle (disregard the extra thickness at the oiling holes). If your clearances are too loose, the only damage will be a loss of some oil control; too tight might mean a spun bearing.

For this engine build, I am using 1.889-inch crank journals and Carrillo rods with the housing bores sized at 2.015 inches. That means the bearing thickness should be approximately 0.062 of an inch for each

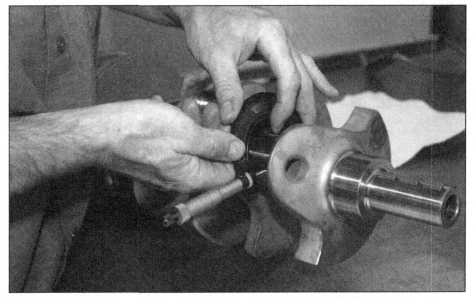

Precise measurement of the crank journals is critical. Even the best cranks exhibit variances of a couple of tenths of one one-thousandth at the oiling holes and in the center of the journal.

If you are using the 1.889-inch "Honda journal" size that's becoming popular in racing, you need to be aware that many of the bearings available in this size aren't chamfered on the outside edge. This is because Honda rods are very wide, making this unnecessary. Chevy V-8 rods are almost exactly the same width, which can leave the bearing rubbing against the radius on the shoulder of the crank journal. To eliminate this problem, Automotive Specialists cuts a radius into the Honda rod bearings on a lathe. It's admittedly low-tech, but it works.

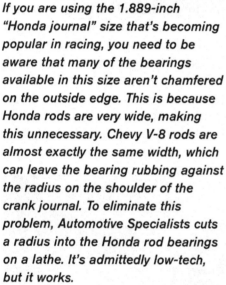

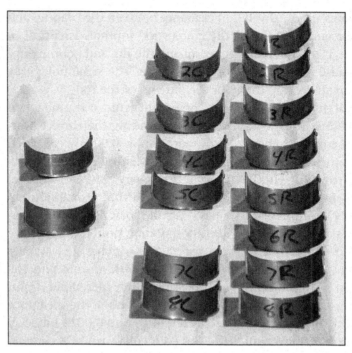

After the big ends of the rods have been honed and the bearings fitted, they should remain matched. You will have the rods apart and back together a few more times before the engine is finally assembled, so go ahead and mark both the rods and bearings with a Sharpie so that you can easily tell which bearing goes with which rod.

shell to give us 0.0019 of an inch of bearing clearance. Simply measuring the bearing shells with a micrometer won't give you the results you are looking for. There is actually little predictability between bearing shell thickness and the final bearing ID diameter once the bearings are installed in the rods.

The only reliable way to determine that your bearing clearance will be correct is to install a bearing shell inside the rod and measure the ID with a dial bore gauge. When measuring the inside diameter of the rod journal, make sure to always measure the bearing diameter 90 degrees from the parting lines (the seam where the upper and lower bearing shells meet). Bearings are thinner near the parting lines to allow greater clearance because the big end of the rod will stretch when changing directions at TDC.

To get the true inside diameter of the bearing in the rod, measure in line with the beam of the rod. This method of measurement requires assembly of all eight rods with bearings, but it is definitely worth the effort. It also means that from this point forward you will need to keep each bearing with the specific connecting rod it has been fitted to. It's a good idea to number each bearing and rod so they won't get mixed up later on.

If the clearances are found to be either too tight or too loose with standard bearing shells, you can use a shell that's manufactured and marked either 0.001 inches thicker or thinner than standard. (Each shell is thicker or thinner by 0.0005 inches, making the total change 0.001 of an inch.) Usually, a full 0.001 of an inch is too much, but you can mix and match shells to achieve the clearance you desire. If you need slightly more clearance you can use half of a standard shell and half of a shell that's 0.001 of an inch under. The result is a bearing ID that is 0.0005 of an inch larger than standard, creating slightly more clearance. If you do go this route, it doesn't really matter if the smaller shell is on the top or bottom; just try to be consistent across all of your rods. Because the bearings are thinner at the parting lines, a ridge between the thicker and thinner shells isn't a problem.

Although there is no bearing, the pin end of the rod should be honed to the same clearance guideline. So for the 0.927-inch diameter pin I am

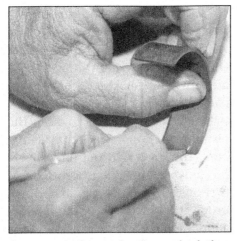

As soon as the engine is cranked, the Sharpie ink will rub off the bearing face, so Dorton also scribes the cylinder number in each bearing tang. If the engine is well built, a set of bearings can be re-used in the rebuild, so this helps ensure they go back into the same rods they came out of.

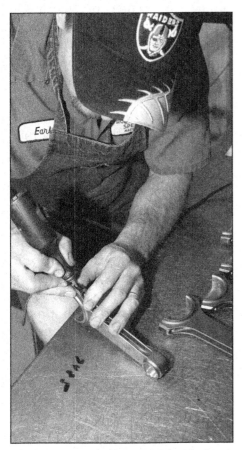

The rods are also marked for their location with an electric scribe.

using, the pin bore should be just over 0.928 of an inch, or between 0.001 and 0.0017 of an inch larger.

Rod Bolt Stretch

One of the keys to making sure your rods survive under the worst racing conditions is to take care of the connecting hardware. It's the two rod bolts that provide all the clamping pressure between the rod and the cap, and they are all that keeps the rod from flying apart under the tremendous inertial forces to which it is subjected. Bolts provide clamping pressure by stretching a small amount as they are twisted into place. Too much stretch and the bolt's tensile strength will be reduced dramatically; too little and the clamping force will be inadequate. This is true for every bolt in every application, but when it comes to connecting rods, the safety zone is razor thin.

The best way to determine bolt stretch is to measure it with a gauge. Fortunately, it is easy to measure stretch with a dedicated rod-bolt stretch gauge. Most manufacturers recommend between 0.005 and 0.007 of an inch of stretch.

You don't have to manually check the stretch of every single bolt. As you pre-fit the rods, check to see how much torque is required to stretch several of the bolts. Each time you fit the rod, the burnishing action between the threads in the bolt and the rod will reduce the amount of torque required to get the same amount of stretch. So each time you fit the rods, check the stretch for the first couple of bolts and note how much torque is required to get the proper amount. After that you can safely torque the rest of the bolts

with relative certainty that they are properly stretched.

Many people believe that torque and stretch are the same thing, but they are not. The quality of the thread lubricant used dramatically affects torque. If you use a relatively poor lubricant, like thin motor oil, a given amount of torque may not

Accurately determining rod stretch is an integral part of preparing bombproof connecting rods. Using a dedicated rod bolt-stretch gauge makes this process very simple. Begin by measuring the bolt in its relaxed state. You will then measure the bolt once it is installed in the rod and monitor its stretch as you add torque in small increments. You cannot depend completely on a torque wrench because each time you re-torque the same bolt in the same rod using the same lubricant, the threads become burnished, and it requires less torque to get the same amount of stretch.

A good rule of thumb when trying to match torque numbers to the correct amount of rod bolt stretch is that 0.0005 of an inch of stretch normally equals about 5 ft-lbs of torque when using a good moly lubricant.

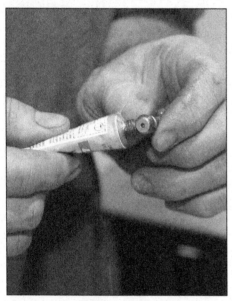

If you are tracking rod bolt stretch, the type of lubricant you use on the bolts isn't critical, but it is still a good idea to be consistent. After checking the stretch on the first couple of bolts and finding the correct torque number, you can now safely put the stretch gauge aside and depend on the torque wrench for the rest. Make sure to lubricate both the threads and the underside of the bolt head.

stretch the bolt enough, and it won't provide enough clamping load. On the other hand, a better lubricant, like a moly-based lube, will make the threads so slick that the same amount of torque may stretch the bolts to the point that they will eventually fail. If you are measuring stretch, it doesn't matter what lubricant you use, because the proper amount of stretch will provide the correct amount of clamping load no matter what.

Pistons

Like connecting rods, there is practically no reason to use a stock piston these days. For racing, where sustained high temperatures and detonation are common, there is really no reason to use any cast or hypereutectic piston at all, unless your rulebook requires it. There are forged aluminum pistons specifically designed for every class you can race, and the weight savings and increased durability are well worth the price.

Race-designed performance pistons can help you shed a lot of weight compared to stock pieces. One of the greatest advantages is the modern slipper skirt design. Compared to stock designs, it looks like it is barely large enough to keep the piston from flopping over inside the bore. The small skirt not only shaves precious weight, but it also reduces friction as it slides up and down inside the cylinder bore. It does allow more "slap" as it rocks inside the bore at BDC (Bottom Dead Center) and at TDC but noise is hardly an issue in racing.

Other big areas of weight savings you should look for in a quality piston are the wristpin size and the location of the pin towers in the piston. Moving the pin towers inboard toward the center of the piston reduces the length of the wristpin and cuts weight. The wristpin, however, must still maintain enough wall thickness (usually 0.165 of an inch on a 0.927-inch-diameter pin) to keep pin flex to a minimum.

Almost all stock car racing rules require a flat-top piston, so that is what I will concentrate on. Of course, even with this limitation, not all flat-top pistons are built the same. Dorton says that dealing with a reputable manufacturer such as JE, Mahle, or Wiseco is key because of the technical knowledge they bring to the table.

No matter how much time is invested in R&D, no engine builder can be thoroughly knowledgeable in every facet of every part that goes into his race engines. Some of this you simply have to leave to the manufacturer and its experience. Manufacturers that are deeply involved in motorsports use what they learn at the highest levels, such as Nextel

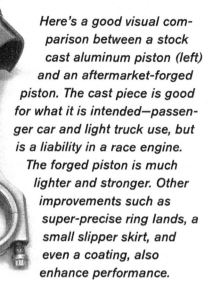

Here's a good visual comparison between a stock cast aluminum piston (left) and an aftermarket-forged piston. The cast piece is good for what it is intended—passenger car and light truck use, but is a liability in a race engine. The forged piston is much lighter and stronger. Other improvements such as super-precise ring lands, a small slipper skirt, and even a coating, also enhance performance.

On uncoated pistons, you can measure piston diameter at the center of the skirt and approximately 1/4 inch above the bottom. You should be aware that pistons with a coated skirt, such as this one, are usually impossible to measure accurately. This means you will just have to depend on your piston manufacturer for accurate measurements.

Cup, to advance the performance of products built for lower racing levels.

A perfect example is the valve pockets in the piston. Just a few years ago, it was standard practice for many engine builders to fly cut valve pockets in the piston tops in order to get the perfect amount of valve clearance for their specific engine package while maximizing compression. The problem is that when a piston manufacturer doesn't know what the

One great way to cut weight and improve strength is to reduce the wristpin length by pulling the piston's pin towers inboard. The pin, however, should still have enough wall thickness to resist flex. If flex does occur, it will quickly lead to the pin galling in the connecting rod's pin bore. Dorton normally uses pins with a wall thickness of at least 0.165 of an inch.

final valve pocket size will be, it has to add in extra material to the underside of the piston top. If the valve pocket the engine builder cuts isn't very deep, this extra material is simply excess weight traveling up and down the cylinder bores at 7,000-plus rpm. Also, the heat generated by any machining processes performed on a piston after the ring lands are cut can cause the lands to distort and harm ring sealing.

Instead, Dorton works with the piston manufacturer to design a custom set of pistons with the correct valve pockets and the minimal amount of aluminum required to withstand the horsepower generated. It is a more expensive option, but one with a large payoff. On a high-rpm racing engine with solid lifters, minimum piston-to-valve clearance should be 0.040 of an inch on the intake and 0.100 of an inch on the exhaust. If you suspect the team you are building the engine for will be experimenting with valve lash or may not lash the valves as often as they should, it is a good idea to open up the minimum clearance even more.

Forged aluminum pistons are almost always constructed from one

of two alloys: 2618 or 4032. Pistons forged from 2618 alloy are generally stronger and more durable because of the reduced silicon content. These pistons require bore clearances between 0.008 and 0.010 of an inch because of the material's greater expansion rates. You will normally only see 2618 alloy in very high-end pistons.

The 4032 aluminum has a higher silicon content. Because of

Pro Tip: Wire Locks

When purchasing pistons with a floating pin arrangement, you will usually have a choice between spiral locks or wire locks. Engine builders have been using spiral locks for years, but they can be tricky to seat properly. Wire locks are gaining popularity because they are easier to install and remove, plus they offer an added level of protection for the piston.

Dorton says that under detonation, the wristpin tries to push the spiral locks out of the groove in the pin bore, due to their flat sides. Because a wire lock is rounded, the chamfer in the wristpin actually pushes the wire lock further up into the pin bore, locking it into place and reducing the potential for damage to the piston.

Wire locks are not only easier to install than more conventional spiral locks, but they also protect the piston body in the event of engine detonation.

the silicon content, it exhibits less thermal expansion than the 2618 alloy. It is strong enough for racing applications and probably more common in most pistons because it is less expensive. With 4032 pistons, Dorton recommends a cylinder bore clearance between 0.004 and 0.005 of an inch.

Balancing

While there are many advantages to running a lightweight reciprocating assembly (crank, rods, pistons, and wristpins), it also requires extra diligence. If one piston/rod combination is either over or under weight relative to the others, if only by a small amount, the relative percentage is much greater than if you are running heavier, stock components. The problem is compounded because your race engine regularly sees RPM levels, for extended periods, that a stock motor cannot even reach. This means that properly balancing your

rotating assembly is even more critical. An engine with even a small balance problem operating at extreme RPMs can create vibrations that will destroy bearings, shear flywheel bolts, or worse.

There are two methods of balancing an engine: externally and

Here, the rod is being weighed to help determine the reciprocating weight. A stationary arm suspends the end that isn't being weighed over the scale.

Earl Mark of Automotive Specialists checks each half of a bob weight individually to make sure that the total weight is correct. He also verifies that both sides of the bob weight are equal.

Piston Coatings

There is virtually no area of the engine that cannot be helped with a coating of some type, and pistons are no exception. You can either purchase pre-coated pistons or you can have them done to your specifications. Here are a few areas to consider:

Skirts: A friction-reducing coating here can have good results. It will reduce friction as the piston moves up and down the cylinder bore and can potentially protect the crosshatch in the bore walls. These coatings work by "holding" on to oil molecules to provide a thin film of oil between the piston skirt and the cylinder wall. Mahle is a leader in this area with its proprietary Grafal skirt coating. If you purchase a set of pistons with coated skirts, be aware that the coating will make it impossible to accurately measure the piston diameter. Although it seems counter to most engine-building practices, you will just have to trust the manufacturer.

Ring Lands: You can help prevent micro-welding the rings to the piston ring lands by adding a diamond-hard coating on the lands. Some manufacturers anodize this area to help minimize micro welding. Anodizing is less effective, but also less expensive.

Piston Top: A heat-resistant coating here will help improve combustion inside the chamber and also help reduce the opportunity for detonation. By coating the top of

Many performance pistons are now available with different coatings. This Mahle piston features a low-friction coating on the skirts that cuts friction and protects both the piston and cylinder bore from scuffing.

the piston so that it absorbs less heat, more of the heat exits out the exhaust port or is absorbed by the cylinder head—where the coolant pulls it away. When the piston runs cooler it is more durable and also less likely to trigger a pre-ignition event.

Piston Underside: Take the opposite approach with the underside of the piston. Here, you can coat the material with a heat dispersant that helps the aluminum radiate off any heat it has absorbed. The oil that is either splashed up onto the piston or purposely sprayed there and carried to the oil cooler will pick up this heat.

internally. An externally balanced engine uses weights on the damper and flywheel to bring the entire rotating assembly into balance. The problem with this, however, is if you ever replace either the damper or flywheel, the engine must be rebalanced. That's why almost all race engines are internally balanced. Weight is either added to or removed from the crank's counterweights at specific locations to bring the entire rotating assembly into balance. Balancing the crank requires expensive machinery, and there are several things you need to know to make sure it's done correctly.

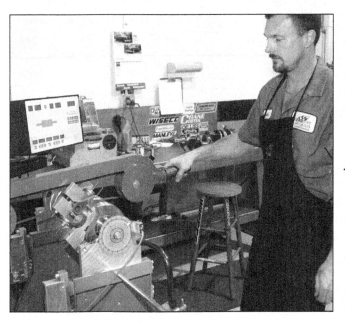

Bob weights, which simulate the weight and motion of two rods, two pistons, and the rest of their associated parts, are attached to each of the crank's four rod journals. When all the bob weights are correctly assembled and installed on the crank, a balancing machine can specify exactly where weight needs to be added or removed.

Instead of drilling holes in the ends of the counterweights, Automotive Specialists prefers to turn down the ends of the counterweights in a lathe. This reduces power-robbing windage by reducing the diameter of the counterweights so they will be less likely to splash in oil collected in the bottom of the pan. It also keeps the outside of the counterweights nice and smooth.

This crank is essentially junk, but you can see the many slugs of Mallory metal that have been pressed into the counterweights. This was the result of an ill-advised effort to match a lightweight crank with piston and rod assemblies that were too heavy.

If your rules allow it, another option for removing metal is to angle the counterweights like this. The idea is that the knifed edges reduce windage in the oil pan.

Balance Versus Overbalance

A crank is balanced when the weight of the rotating portion of the assembly (the crank, the rod bearings, and the big end of the rod) matches the weight of the reciprocating portion (the pistons, wristpins, locks, rings, and the small end of the rod) plus a couple grams thrown in to account for clinging oil. As already noted, the most common method for balancing the assembly is either to remove weight from the crank's counterweights by cutting material away or by adding weight in the form of Mallory metal plugs. Mallory metal is a tungsten alloy that is several times denser, and therefore heavier, than the steel a crank is made from.

A 50 percent balance is when the bob weights used on the crank balancing machine are equal to 100 percent of the rotating weight and 50 percent of the reciprocating weight. (For more information on bob weights and how to calculate them, see the "Calculating Balance Weights" sidebar.) This will eliminate most engine vibrations but isn't always effective for high-rpm applications.

Overbalancing is when you balance the crank with 100 percent of the rotating weight and more than 50 percent of the reciprocating weight. Typically, 51 or 52 percent of the reciprocating weight works best for short-track racing engines. You don't want too much overbalance percentage because a circle track engine will sweep through a wide RPM band from the corner to the end of the straight. The goal is to find the balance percentage that most effectively eliminates vibrations in your racing RPM range.

Piston Rings

The act of gapping rings is one of the most tedious aspects of building any engine, and most engine builders will tell you it's their least favorite part. Still, it must be done. Most professional engine builders use a powered ring filer—Goodson sells a popular one. They are the quickest and most accurate option available. But they are a significant investment and likely are too costly for people who aren't building engines for a living.

A crank-style ring filer is a more economical option and works well if you don't mind working slowly. You must be careful to only make small cuts on the rings because you can't put material back if you grind away too much. It may take a little practice to get a smooth, perpendicular cut on the ring.

Most performance packages use 1/16, 1/16, 3/16 ring sets. For all-out racing applications, consider moving to thinner rings. Generally, these were originally designed for smaller import motors and are measured in metric sizes. You can get good oil control with less friction using .043-inch first and second rings with a 3-mm oil ring. When using a moly top ring with a ductile iron second ring, you will want your rings to be gapped at 0.022 of an inch for the first ring and 0.016 of an inch for the second.

Calculating Balance Weights

Bob weights are actual weights that are attached to the crank's rod journals to simulate the weight of the rod, rod bearing, piston, wristpin, pin locks, and clinging oil. Calculating bob weights to match your engine components isn't difficult, but it does require a little math and some time spent with a set of scales. Here's the complete list of what must be weighed before determining your bob weights for zero-balancing a crank.

Rotating Weight:
--Big end of rod (including fastening hardware)
--Rod Bearing
--Oil (normally estimated at four grams)

Reciprocating Weight
--Piston
--Wristpin
--Pin locks (not applicable if using press-fit pins)
--Small end of rod
--Piston rings
--Oil

Bob Weight = Rotating Weight + (Reciprocating Weight x .50)

If you want a 51 percent overbalance, simply replace .50 in the equation with .51.

Bob weights attach to the crank's rod journals to simulate the weight of the piston and rod. That's why when an engine builder says he was able to "cut the bob weight," it's always a good thing. It means a lighter rotating assembly.

A crank-style ring grinder, like this one from Powerhouse Products, can do a good job if you are willing to take your time. There is no way to measure how much material you are removing, so you have to cut a little at a time and check your ring gap in the cylinder bore often.

Before you can accurately measure ring gap with a feeler gauge you have to make sure the ring is parallel to the deck. The easiest way to do this is to place the ring in the bore, near the top. Then, place another ring in the top or second ring land of a piston and insert the piston in the bore upside down. This will push the ring you are fitting down the cylinder bore. When the ring on the piston catches on the deck of the block, the face of the piston—and the ring inside the bore—will be parallel to the deck.

There really isn't much power to be gained from going tighter, and these gaps protect you from scrubbing the rings against the cylinder walls in the event of overheating. Dorton says he has dyno tested top ring gaps as open as 0.032 of an inch and not seen much of a power loss on the dyno, although you probably will notice excess smoke from the tailpipes.

Dorton normally gaps oil rings to 0.010 of an inch. Like the top ring, you can live with as much as 0.025 of an inch gap without significant performance loss. And again, too loose is better than too tight. An oil ring gapped too tight means cylinder wall damage and potentially micro welding the ring to the piston's ring land. As before, too loose just means a little less oil control.

Measure the ring gap by placing the ring in the bore it will wind up in upon final assembly and use a feeler gauge to determine the width of the gap. Before you can accurately measure ring gap with a feeler gauge you have to be able to make sure the ring

You must ensure every ring you gap is installed in the bore you gapped it for. The best way to do this is to place your rings on a rack marked for each cylinder in the engine immediately after it has been gapped. Nothing fancy is required here. This rack is homemade, but it does the job perfectly.

is parallel to the deck. The easiest way to do this is to place the ring in the bore, near the top. Then, place another ring in the top or second ring land of a piston and insert the piston in the bore upside down. This

will push the ring you are fitting down the cylinder bore. When the ring on the piston catches on the deck of the block, the face of the piston—and the ring inside the bore—will be parallel to the deck.

Once you have the correct gap, use a very fine file to remove any burrs created by the grinding process from the ends of the rings. Be very careful not to round off the corners of the rings, as this will allow combustion gasses to leak past. All you want to do is knock off any rough edges.

Pro Tip: Take Advantage of Oil Ring Tension

Through years of research, Dorton has learned to gain power from the oil rings in a manner that few other engine builders know about. By carefully controlling the amount of tension between the oil rings and the cylinder walls, Dorton has found a couple of horsepower on the dyno without any appreciable loss of oil control.

Interestingly, oil ring tension isn't determined solely by ring gap as it is on the top two rings. The oil rings are also affected by how the expander fits in the cylinder bore and the radial thickness of the oil rings themselves. The radial thickness is the distance between the inside edge and the outside edge of the ring, and Dorton says the radial thickness of the oil rings he uses can vary between 0.096 to 0.106 of an inch. The variance seems to come between production runs, so you should see some consistency between sets. Because the ID of the oil ring sits inside the expander rail, a ring with a greater radial thickness will exhibit more power-robbing tension than a thinner ring—even if the gap is the same.

Begin by measuring the radial thickness of all your oil rings. Keep the thinnest and save the rings with a greater radial thickness for a later rebuild. Dorton says he regularly has to go through two sets of rings to get a matched set of eight. Of course, he can afford to do this with the number of engines leaving his shop. If you are only building a single engine, try checking with a local engine builder or the machine shop that prepped your block to see if they would be willing to swap a few rings.

You can also check for variances in your expander rings. A properly sized expander ring will fit in the cylinder bore so that the ends just butt without buckling the ring. There should be enough tension, however, that the ring will hold itself in place inside the cylinder bore. You cannot gap an expander ring, but if you have one that is too small inside the bore (it won't hold itself inside the cylinder bore), it could be paired to work well with an oil ring that has a greater radial thickness.

You can actually feel the difference in a well-matched set of low-tension oil rings. Install both oil rings with the expander on a piston that has been installed on a rod and insert the piston into a dry cylinder bore upside down. Using the connecting rod as a handle, slide the piston up and down inside the bore and feel the resistance. Now try the same thing with a set of oil rings with a greater radial thickness matched to the same expander ring and notice the difference.

Ring tension isn't only controlled by the size of the ring gap. Because the ID of the two oil rings fit around a portion of the expander ring, how tightly the expander fits in the cylinder bore affects ring tension.

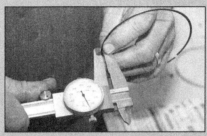

The radial thickness of a ring cannot be changed. Dorton says he commonly sees as much as 0.010 of an inch variance in a single set, so you may need to go through a couple packs to achieve a matched set. Rings with less radial thickness will produce less tension inside the cylinder bore.

Although you cannot gap expander rings, you can find some that do have a gap inside the bore, such as this one. Match these with oil rings that have a greater radial thickness.

You can actually feel the difference in drag when ring tension is decreased. Install a set of oil rings with less radial thickness on a piston and rod and insert the piston upside down inside a dry cylinder bore. Feel how much effort it takes to move it up and down inside the bore. Now do the same thing with a set of oil rings that have a greater radial thickness matched with the same expander ring. As long as they are gapped correctly (around 0.010 of an inch) the thinner set of rings burns up less of the engine's power and should still provide good oil control.

Installing the Crank

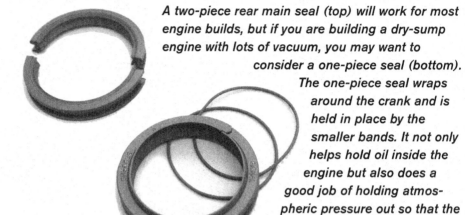

A two-piece rear main seal (top) will work for most engine builds, but if you are building a dry-sump engine with lots of vacuum, you may want to consider a one-piece seal (bottom). The one-piece seal wraps around the crank and is held in place by the smaller bands. It not only helps hold oil inside the engine but also does a good job of holding atmospheric pressure out so that the oil pump can create a vacuum inside the crankcase.

Crank installation begins by placing the main bearings in the housing bore. Ensure all components are absolutely clean and free of grit before proceeding. Next, place the bearing shells in the block so that the tangs on the backsides of the bearings fit into the slots in the block. The grooved bearing shells go into the block side of the housing bore, while the shells with the smooth bearing face go into the cap side. On a Chevy small-block, the first four bearings are interchangeable. The fifth bearing, which goes in the rear main, is the thrust bearing, which has the crankshaft thrust face.

Apply a thin film of gasket sealer or silicone to the back of both halves of the seal and then slide it into position with the lip pointing inward. Make sure to "clock" the seal, or press it in off-center a bit, so that the parting lines for the seal aren't lined up with the parting line of the cap or two-piece seal adaptor, to keep oil from seeping between the combined parting lines.

Apply a liberal amount of assembly lubricant to all the bearing surfaces and a thin coat of oil or high-pressure lube to the rear main seal. You can then lay the crank in place. Make sure the crank rotates smoothly without binding.

When installing the main caps on the block—whether test fitting or final assembly—they should be a tight fit into the registers on the block. You can use a small rubber mallet to tap them into place. Resist the urge to use the cap bolts to pull the caps into position as this can damage both the threads in the block and the caps.

Make sure to lubricate the threads of the main bolts or studs with oil or high-pressure lube before you begin the torquing process. Torque the first four main caps in 25 ft-lb increments until you reach the bolt manufacturer's specifications. For bolts lubricated with motor oil, it is 70 ft-lbs for the inside set and 65 ft-lbs for the outside bolts on a four-bolt cap. Now, move the crank back and forth to set the thrust face on your thrust bearing. You can do this by tapping the crank a few times with a dead-blow hammer or by wedging a large screwdriver between one of the main caps and a counter-weight on the crank. Once you have done this, torque the rear main cap in the same manner as the others.

Using a dial indicator with a magnetic base, check the crank's endplay. Set the indicator to measure horizontal movement at the nose of the crank, and pry the crank back and forth with a screwdriver. Although it isn't as accurate, you can also measure endplay by inserting a feeler gauge between the crank and the thrust bearing. On most engines you want between 0.005 and 0.010 of an inch of play. If there isn't enough clearance, first check to make sure the upper and lower thrust faces of the two bearing halves are properly aligned. Small amounts of endplay can be added by gently lapping the thrust face of the bearing on wet, ultra-fine sandpaper laid on a flat surface. If there is too much clearance you most likely have a poorly ground crank that will need to be replaced.

Rod and Piston Assembly

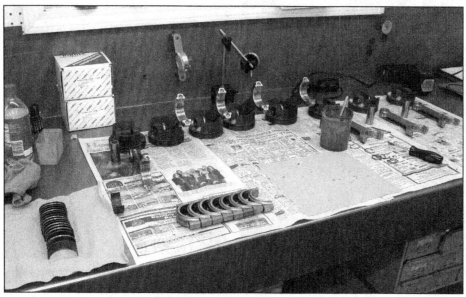

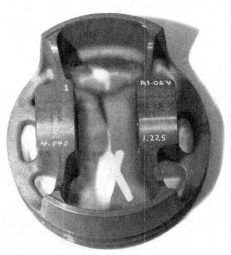

When you begin the rod and piston assembly process, make sure you have a good, clean area for working. Ideally, it should offer plenty of space to lay out everything in an organized manner. Organize the pistons in the order they will go into the engine, ensuring that the valve reliefs in the piston tops match the valve orientation for the cylinder it will be installed in. Then, match the rods to the pistons so that the rods are oriented with the chamfered side facing the closest fillet on the crank.

Along with marking the rods and bearings, Dorton also marks each piston with critical build data. This information includes the cylinder number, cylinder bore size, the compression height, and an engine ID number. Doing this makes the information readily available at teardown and rebuild time.

Before assembly, be sure both the wristpins and pin bores are generously lubricated. Dorton uses Red Line Synthetic assembly lube because it is a quality lubricant. Its thickness ensures it will still be there when the engine is cranked.

Use a small, flat-blade screwdriver when installing the wire locks on full-floater pins. Use caution here, as you do not want to scar the piston. Be careful to properly orient the rods on the pistons. You should already know which cylinder each piston and rod will be going into. Be sure the chamfered side of the rod journal faces the fillet of the crank.

Install the rings on the pistons, beginning with the oil rails. Some piston rings have a top and a bottom (the top is usually marked with a dimple). Be sure all rings are correctly oriented.

If you are using spiral locks to hold the wristpin in place, use the same screwdriver to slowly walk the lock into place. Be sure the lock is fully seated in the piston groove.

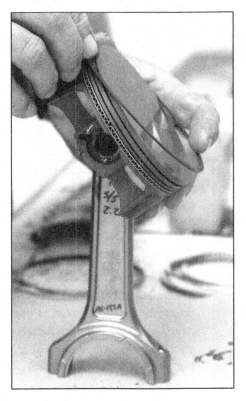

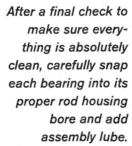

Orient the ring gaps for the two compression rings so that they are 180 degrees from each other. This will limit power-robbing blow-by.

After a final check to make sure everything is absolutely clean, carefully snap each bearing into its proper rod housing bore and add assembly lube.

Wipe down the cylinder bores with lacquer thinner to make sure there are no contaminants, and then apply a thin film of oil.

Coat the rings and the piston skirts with oil to protect the piston and rings from galling at start up.

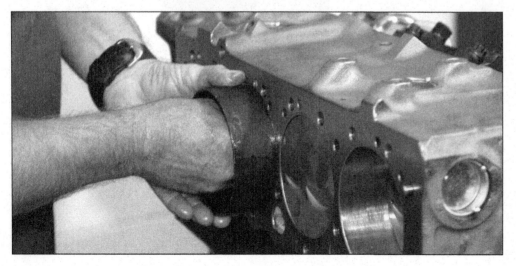

Install the ring compressor over the piston and position the rod and piston—correctly oriented so that the chamfer on the big end of the rod faces the crank fillet—in the cylinder bore. Make sure the crank journal for the cylinder you are working on is at BDC. With low-tension rings you should be able to use your fingers to slide the piston into the bore, but you can also tap the top of the piston with the handle of a hammer.

Check rod bearing side clearance by inserting a feeler gauge between the two rod caps on one crank journal. Maximum clearance should be no more than 0.015 of an inch, while the minimum clearance should be at least 0.008 of an inch. Too little clearance usually means a bearing is rubbing against the crank fillet, while too much is often a sign of an improperly ground crank.

Once all the piston rings are inside the bore, reach around and pull the rod/piston assembly down until the rod bearing is fully seated on the crank journal. Install the appropriate rod cap (with rod bearing installed) and finger tighten the bolts. The rod bolts should be coated with the same lube you used when checking rod-bearing clearance. Continue until all eight pistons and rods are in position.

From your earlier work measuring rod-bearing clearance, you should know approximately how many ft-lbs of torque are required to achieve the proper rod bolt stretch. Still, you should check again on at least the first connecting rod. Begin by measuring your rod bolt length in a relaxed state and then torque to 10 ft-lbs less than the proper stretch number you found earlier. Measure stretch and continue to torque in 5 ft-lb increments until you achieve 0.005 to 0.007 of an inch of stretch. If you need to add five more foot-pounds of torque, make sure to first loosen the bolt and re-torque to your new setting. Do not simply add five more foot-pounds, because a torque wrench isn't accurate when used in that manner. Try that torque number again on your next bolt and check the stretch. If the torque number provides the correct amount of stretch consistently on two to four rod bolts, you can set aside the stretch gauge. At this point, you can confidently torque the remaining rod bolts to the number you have found, which is usually somewhere between 40 to 55 ft-lbs. This will vary depending on rod bolt size and the lubricant used.

CYLINDER HEADS AND THE VALVETRAIN

Possibly the most critical component to making power in any Chevy engine is the valvetrain. The components you choose and how you assemble them will determine the valvetrain's overall stability, durability, and, of course, how much air and fuel it allows into the combustion chambers. For our purposes, you must also consider the cylinder heads as part of the valvetrain. They determine the geometry of the system by providing the mounting points for the rocker arms and seats for the springs, and they supply the sealing surface for the valves.

Cylinder Head Machine Work

As with the block, proper machining, inspection, and cleaning of your cylinder heads is critical to a successful engine build. And also like the block, many of the machining processes require very specialized equipment that makes it extremely difficult to do the work yourself.

Decking

Decking is the process of machining off a portion of the surface of the heads that mate with the block. This ensures a square, flat surface to provide proper sealing with the head gasket. Decking can also be used to increase compression by reducing the size of the combustion chambers.

An offshoot technique of the decking process is known as angle milling. Angle milling is the process

of angle cutting the deck of the head to reduce the valve angle. By cutting more material off of the exhaust side of the deck of the heads, you can reduce the valve angle by a couple of degrees. For example, a 23-degree Chevy head can be angle milled to give a valve angle of 21 or 20 degrees without making other drastic changes. The shallower valve angle improves flow into the engine by reducing the shrouding effect around the valves.

Instead of decking the cylinder head parallel with the original surface, you can have the deck angle milled. This removes more material from the exhaust side of the head than the intake side, allowing you to modify the valve angle. Essentially, this means you can "stand the valves up," or reduce their angle in relation to the pistons. Creating a shallower valve angle makes a standard 23-degree cylinder head flow more like a high-end 18-degree head. This results in less valve shrouding, which means more air and fuel make it into the combustion chambers.

One difficulty that comes with angle milling is that it changes the way the heads sit on the block. Specifically, the angle of the intake face of the heads (where the intake manifold mates to the head) is changed. To fit heads that have been angle milled, you will have to re-machine either the intake manifold or the intake face of the cylinder heads. The head bolt holes (shown here) will also have to be slotted to allow the head bolts to thread into the block.

Keith Dorton uses a milling machine to open up the pushrod holes, and this photo shows you just how much clearance can be added. If you attempt this on a mill with cast iron heads, use a cutter that's at least 5/8 of an inch in diameter. This reduces the chances of breaking the cutter on the hard cylinder head material. You can achieve the same results with a die grinder. A nice side benefit of this procedure is the removal of a bit of weight off the top of the heads.

One operation you can perform yourself is to open up the pushrod holes in the cylinder heads for additional clearance. In this stock Bow Tie head, you can see how small the square pushrod holes are. They also have a large amount of casting "slag" around them. This may prevent the increased lateral pushrod movement that is needed when using high-ratio rocker arms.

Of course, angle milling a pair of cylinder heads does require further changes. Because the way the head sits on the block has changed, you will likely have to slot the head bolt holes for the head bolts to fit the threads in the block.

You will also need to machine the surfaces where the manifold and head mate to get them to match up again. Special care must be taken to make sure the intake runners in the manifold and head haven't moved out of alignment. Finally, you may also need to add more clearance for the changed pushrod angles. When done well, angle milling is a good way to add power in a class where your choice of racing heads is limited. But when done poorly, angle milling can cause more harm than good.

Valveguides

Many aftermarket performance heads ship with bronze valveguides installed. All aluminum cylinder heads must have either bronze or iron guides. The bronze reduces the chance of the valvestem galling to the wall of the guide. If you are using stock-style heads and a high-lift cam, you may want to add bronze guide inserts.

Whether you are running bronze guides or using cast iron, the guides must be honed to the correct tolerance. For an aluminum head with bronze valveguides, that should usually be around 0.0012 of an inch on the intake and 0.0015 of an inch for the exhaust, which sees more heat. For a cast iron head with iron guides you can get by with 0.0015 of an inch of clearance on both. An additional benefit of properly honed guides is that the guide walls will have a nice crosshatch pattern just like the cylinder bores. The crosshatch helps retain a tiny bit of oil between the valvestem and the guide to reduce the chances of galling.

Spring Seats

One of the ways high-performance springs normally get their extra strength is by being wound to a larger diameter than their stock counterparts. So when using stock or stock-replacement heads, it can often be necessary to re-cut the valvespring pockets to a larger diameter to accommodate your specific springs. Valve seats are sometimes cut deeper into the heads to increase the spring's installed height without having to use valves with longer (and heavier) stems.

When cutting spring seats, it is critical that your machinist doesn't cut too far and break into the water jacket. On some heads, just widening the spring seat to match the diameter of your racing springs will intrude into the water jackets. In such a case, shims must be used to raise the original seat.

Screw-In Rocker Studs

Stock heads use press-in rocker studs because they are more economical. These are fine with lightweight stock springs, but the extra force created by a high-pressure racing valvespring can pull the stud out of the head. As a general guideline, any time you are using valvesprings with more than 100 lbs of seat pressure, the heads should be tapped to accept screw-in studs.

It is possible to cut the threads with a hand tap, but it isn't advisable. When cutting the threads by hand, there is no way to guarantee that the alignment is correct. Any error here can change valvetrain geometry and lead to part failures.

Valve Seats

The seats for the intake and exhaust ports provide the sealing surface for the valves. They should also be considered part of the port and vital to ensuring the greatest amount of air and fuel are able to flow into the combustion chambers. The seats are, in fact, the transition between the port and the combustion chamber.

Most rulebooks allow a competition three-angle valve job on the seats. The standard angles in this situation are 45 degrees for the actual seal, with a 30-degree angle above it (the entrance to the combustion chamber) and a 60-degree angle below it (between the seat and the port). This is a vast improvement over a stock valve job that employs just a single angle. But it can still be improved.

Use extreme caution when cutting spring seats. Larger-diameter performance springs require wider spring seats, but cutting them at the same depth as the original seats can cause you to break into the water jacket and ruin the head. In this situation, Dorton cuts the seat at a higher level than the original seat and then uses a shim to level everything up. The shim will change the spring's installed height, so remember to take this into account.

If you are upgrading stock cylinder heads, it can be tempting to pull the rocker studs and tap the holes yourself for high-grade threaded rocker studs. Resist that temptation; any small change in the angle of the stud can have dire consequences on the valvetrain. Pay your machinist to prepare your cylinder heads for threaded rocker studs.

Jeff Dorton cuts seats on a new cylinder head. Even when using the "standard" angles (a 45-degree seat sandwiched between 60- and 30-degree angles), he says that flow can be improved by cutting in radiused transitions between each angle.

Rather than leaving sharp edges between the angles, use a cutter to create a radius that blends the angle changes gently to further increase air and fuel flow. A slightly different strategy is warranted for the exhaust seats in highly efficient combustion chambers. Here, the goal is to guide the spent hydrocarbons out of the chamber and into the exhaust ports. This is often best achieved by eliminating the top angle and utilizing a radius to blend the chamber roof into the 45-degree valve seat.

Of course, extensive testing on flow benches has shown that the most efficient valve angles are dependent on total valve lift. If you are racing a class that limits total valve lift or requires no more than the stock lift numbers, you can consider flattening out the valve seat. With lower valve lift there is less room for the air and fuel to get around the head of the valve. In this scenario, the valve seat angle is approximately 30

degrees with 45- and 15-degree angles above and below. This works because the natural tendency of both air and liquids is to follow a surface. The shallower angles help guide the air/fuel charge along the sides of the combustion chamber and around the head of the valve.

In high-lift valvetrains—generally above 0.600 of an inch total lift—the opposite holds true. When the valve is far away from the valve seat, it only requires a small change in direction of the air/fuel charge to clear the valve. Now, the most efficient method for getting the air/fuel charge into the combustion chamber is to use taller (numerically larger) angles, which sends the incoming charge more directly into the chamber. The actual angles often vary depending on the engine builder, but they are usually somewhere around 70, 55, and 40 degrees.

One drawback of using such extreme valve angles is that it is

really hard on the seat and valve. Instead of dropping the valve onto the seat, which is the case with a 45-degree seat, the valve is now actually wedging itself into the seat. As a result, the lifespan of both the seat and the valve is significantly shortened. If you choose to use large valve angles, be prepared for frequent cylinder head rebuilds.

Valvespring Seat Versus Nose Pressures

When discussing the strength of a set of valvesprings, you will often hear the terms "on the seat" and "over the nose." These refer to the two main positions of the spring during engine operation. "On the seat" refers to the pressure the spring is exerting on the valve when it is closed (when the valve is sitting on the valve seat). There should always be pressure on the spring even when the valve is closed, or else the valve will bounce back open when it contacts the seat. If you do have valve bounce, you not only stand the chance of damaging both the valve and the cylinder head, you also lose cylinder pressure, which costs you power.

As a general rule, the higher the RPM range, the more seat pressure the engine requires to eliminate the chance of valve bounce. Good seat pressure helps transfer heat from the valve to the head. In the case of classes requiring stock hydraulic lifters, it also exerts enough pressure on the lifter's plunger to prevent the lifter from pumping up and holding the valve open.

"Over the nose" is the spring pressure at maximum lift, when the lifter is riding over the nose of the cam. The inertial forces acting upon a lifter as a performance cam raises it can be quite drastic. The valvespring must have sufficient nose pressure both to decelerate the valve as the cam reaches max lift and then close the valve at the speed determined by the backside of the cam lobe. If the spring isn't strong enough, the lifter will loft, or lose contact with the cam lobe. When the spring is finally able to overcome the lifter's inertia, it will close the gaps in the valvetrain violently, sending a damaging, power-robbing shockwave throughout the system.

Unlike seat pressure, which is based on a specific installed height and is easy to determine, a spring's pressure over the nose is influenced by multiple factors. These are the spring's height at max lift, seat pressure, and spring rate.

Adjusting Spring Pressures

Properly matching a spring's seat and nose pressures to the needs of your valvetrain is critical. Unfortu-

The easiest way to check installed spring height is with a tool appropriately named a "height micrometer." Install the micrometer in the place of a spring on a valve with the retainer and locks you plan to use. Extend the micrometer until the valve is fully seated and check the reading. This is your installed height.

nately, there is no way to tell you exactly what is needed for every possible engine package. Heavier hydraulic lifters require stronger springs. Roller cams can handle more radical lobe profiles, which also require stronger springs. Springs secured by titanium retainers require

less nose pressure than springs secured by heavier steel retainers. And the list goes on.

You already know what happens if the valvesprings are too light, but too much spring pressure can also cause problems. Excessive spring pressure causes elevated wear from

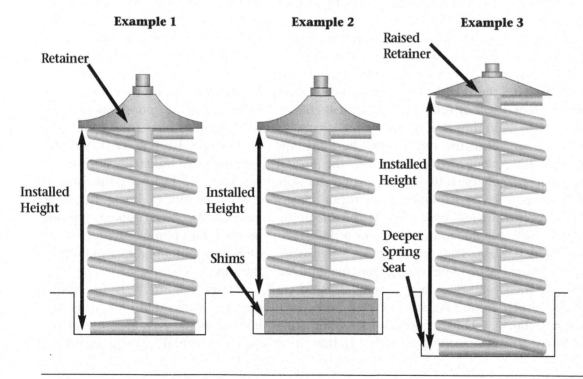

Example 1   **Example 2**   **Example 3**

Retainer

Raised Retainer

Installed Height

Installed Height

Installed Height

Shims

Deeper Spring Seat

A valvespring's installed height is the distance between the bottom of the retainer and the spring seat on the cylinder head, as shown in Example 1. You can decrease the installed height by inserting shims between the spring seat and the spring, as in Example 2. Increasing the installed height can be achieved by machining the head to lower the spring seat, switching to a retainer that locates the top of the spring higher, or both, as in Example 3.

Determining spring pressures at installed height (on the seat) or at full lift (over the nose) requires a spring checker such as this. They are expensive but can be a good investment if you plan to maintain your own engines. By using the height micrometer, you can see exactly how much pressure the spring will be exerting on the valve when it is closed.

One of the keys to improving valve control is to reduce the mass of different components in the system. For years, one of the best ways to do this has been with titanium valvespring retainers. Unfortunately, they are also expensive and illegal in many rulebooks. Recently, new designs are allowing steel retainers (shown here) to be as light as those made from titanium. At the time this book went to press, these new designs require special machining processes, which means they are nearly as expensive as titanium, but the prices should start dropping soon.

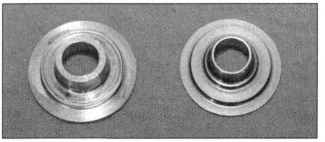

Another advantage for steel over titanium is steel's better wear characteristics. On the left is a titanium valvespring retainer that Dorton pulled from an engine during a rebuild. You can see the wear that the retainer has suffered because it is significantly softer than the spring material. This retainer is headed for the trashcan. On the right is a steel retainer that has also been pulled during a rebuild after an equivalent amount of track time. The steel retainer shows no signs of wear and will be re-installed on the engine.

friction on both the cam lobes and lifters. This situation can also cause the pushrods to flex as they try to move the rocker arms against spring pressure. When this happens, it delays the timing for intake and exhaust valve opening, which hurts power.

The spring's installed height is measured when the spring is installed on the head and the valve is properly seated. It is the dimension between the top of the spring seat on the cylinder head and the bottom of the retainer, specifically the surface that the top of the spring contacts. Spring manufactur-

ers give the seat pressure for their springs at a specific installed height. Raising or lowering the installed height can decrease or increase the seat pressure, respectively.

Increasing the installed height means either lowering the seat location on the head (by machining away material) or raising the location of the spring retainer. This can be done either by switching to valves with longer stems, using offset valve locks that change the retainer's position relative to the valvestem, or using different retainers that locate the top of the spring higher. Its best to avoid switching

stem lengths to influence spring heights, as this also changes the rocker arm height and requires changing pushrod lengths, which can lead to geometry problems.

Decreasing the installed height to raise the seat pressure can be accomplished by opposite measures. You can raise the spring seat on the cylinder head by inserting shims between the spring and seat, and you can lower the retainer height with offset locks or by using a different style retainer. Again, changing the valvestem length without checking how it will affect the rocker arm geometry is a mistake.

Valvespring Coil Bind

When changing either the installed height or max lift, you should always check to make sure the spring won't go into coil bind. Coil bind is when the spring is compressed so far that its coils touch one another and it can be compressed no further. Uncontrolled coil bind will lead to a broken spring or bent pushrod. This is a concern when changing to a higher lift cam or higher ratio rocker arms.

Most manufacturers provide minimum spring heights at maximum valve lift for every spring, but it is a good idea to check this yourself. With a spring installed on a cylinder head, use a spring-compressing tool to compress the spring until it goes into full bind. Now, measure the distance between the bottom of the retainer to the spring seat. The recommended safety margin is 0.060 of an inch, so add this to the height of the spring at coil bind. Subtract this number from your installed height. This is your maximum spring travel—which is also your maximum valve lift for this setup.

If you desire more valve lift than your maximum spring travel will allow you need to increase your installed height. Often, this change will make your seat pressure too low, which means new springs will be required. When you are checking the valvesprings for coil bind issues, it is also a good time to check the entire valve assembly to make sure there also won't be clearance issues between the retainer and valve seal when the valve is at full lift.

Calculating Compression

Calculating engine compression is simple enough: It's the ratio of the volume of the combustion chamber and bore when the piston is at BDC (Bottom Dead Center) versus when it is at TDC (Top Dead Center).

Before you can calculate compression you have to know your engine's displacement. The easy approach is just to use the displacement listed for your block in the catalog, but you need more precision than that. Displacement is defined simply as the area swept by the top of the piston as it moves up or down the cylinder bore one time. It does not include any area above TDC, meaning the combustion chamber. Let's take stock Chevy small-block dimensions (4.00-inch bore and 3.48-inch stroke) as an example.

The formula for calculating displacement for one cylinder is:
Bore x Bore x Stroke x 0.7854 = Cubic Inches

In our example, the calculation works out like this:
4 x 4 x 3.48 x 0.7854 = 43.73 Cubic Inches

The total displacement is eight times 43.73 or 349.84 cubic inches. That strange number—0.7854—is simply a constant that converts everything to cubic inches and incorporates π, because we are dealing with a cylindrical volume.

Calculating Compression Ratio

Calculating the displacement is easy. All you need to know is bore and stroke. But to understand the compression ratio you also need to take into account all of the area that remains in the combustion chamber when the piston is at TDC. Easy enough, that's just the combustion chamber volume, right? Unfortunately, that's only part of the equation. The calculation for determining compression ratio works out like this:

(D + PV + DC + G + CC) / (PV + DC + G + CC) = CR

CR = Compression Ratio
D = Displacement
PV = Piston Volume
DC = Deck Clearance Volume
G = Gasket Volume
CC = Combustion Chamber Volume

Variables that affect piston volume are domes, dishes (which include valve pockets), and the side clearance (which also includes the open area inside the top ring groove that isn't occupied by the ring). If you are purchasing off-the-shelf pistons, the manufacturer can tell you these volumes. For instance, a 5-cc dome on the top of a piston will increase compression ratio versus a flat-top piston. Likewise, large valve pockets will decrease compression. We'll get into the calculations later.

When it comes to understanding compression, it is less critical—but still important—to know the piston's side clearance. Side clearance is the area between the side of the piston and the cylinder bore. It extends from the top edge of the piston down to the top ring. A little-known fact about most racing pistons is that the diameter of the piston above the top ring land is smaller than the rest of the piston. This is because the top of the piston receives tremendous heat from combustion, and the extra clearance is required to allow for expansion. Because racing pistons try to minimize the ring depth, the volume of the side clearance is minimal. Most sanctioning bodies that attempt to regulate compression ratio will allow 1cc for piston side clearance.

Deck Clearance Volume is determined by the distance between the top of the piston at TDC and the deck of the block. Normally on racing engines, the piston at TDC is between .005 and .020 of an inch below the deck. It is possible that the piston has a zero deck height (even with the deck of the block) or even extends above the block, in which case it should be given a negative value in our equation. You can measure deck clearance using a bridge and dial indicator with the piston at TDC. Be aware that pistons, especially a cold piston in a cold bore, can rock on its pin, so always measure along the axis of the piston pin.

The formula for determining Deck Clearance Volume is similar to displacement:

Bore x Bore x 0.7854 x Distance between Piston and Deck at TDC = DC

If the piston in our example is 0.020 of an inch down in the bore at TDC, then the equation works out like this:

4 x 4 x 0.7854 x 0.020 = 0.2513 Cubic Inches

Gasket Volume is almost exactly the same. It is simply the volume contained in the compressed height of the gasket. Properly torqued between the head and engine block, a compressed gasket is normally between 0.005 and 0.015 of an inch thick. The compressed thickness value can be provided by the manufacturer and is usually found in the catalog. Calculate gasket volume exactly like you would deck clearance volume except use the figure for the compressed gasket thickness in place of your value for the distance between the piston and deck at TDC.

4 x 4 x 0.7854 x 0.015 = 0.1885 Cubic Inches

Our last variable is Combustion Chamber Volume. There is no doubt this is the area that has the biggest impact on compression ratio. Most combustion chambers for racing small blocks are between 60 and 90 cubic *centimeters* (see how to convert this measurement on page 52), which is huge compared to the 5-cc dishes in the piston. Manufacturers will tell you what the chamber volume should be, but that number is rarely accurate once the head has been machined. Many machining operations affect chamber volume, including the depth at which the seats are cut, cutting of the chamber walls to unshroud the valves, angle milling the head, and decking the surface. The best way to be absolutely sure of your chamber volumes is to cc the heads. This is a simple process that I show in detail in the accompanying photographs.

It is easy to find the combined piston and deck clearance volumes using the same method as for cc'ing the heads. If you have cut your own valve pockets, fly-cut the top of the piston, or simply just want to check things for yourself, this is a worthwhile procedure. Install at least one piston (with its top ring installed) and rod on the crank in the block. Move the piston part way down into the bore and wipe a small amount of grease or Vaseline around the inside top edge of the bore. Move the piston to TDC and wipe away the excess grease above the piston top. What is left should seal the crevice volume, which is the area between the side of the piston and the bore above the top ring. With the piston sealed, you can now use your burette of fluid to cc the piston at TDC just as you would the combustion chamber.

Now that all of our variables have been defined, let's work on a few examples. Continuing with our now-familiar 4-inch bore and 3.48-inch stroke, let's assume you have the following variables:

Calculating Compression continued...

- 5-cc piston valve pockets
- piston height at TDC is .020 of an inch below the deck
- .015 of an inch compressed gasket thickness
- 70-cc combustion chambers

From the earlier calculations, you know:
- Displacement for one cylinder is 43.73 cubic inches.
- Deck clearance volume is 0.2513 cubic inches.
- Gasket volume is 0.1885 cubic inches.

But the piston and combustion chamber volumes are in cubic centimeters, which must be converted to inches. The formula to convert cubic centimeters to cubic inches is:

cc's x 0.0610237 = Cubic Inches

That means that the 5-cc piston volume converts to 0.305 cubic inches and the 70-cc combustion chamber converts to 4.272 cubic inches. Now you can plug these figures into our formula:

(D + PV + DC + G + CC) / (PV + DC + G + CC) = CR

(43.73 + 0.305 + 0.2513 + 0.1885 + 4.272) /
(0.305 + 0.2513 + 0.1885 + 4.272) = CR
48.7468 / 5.0168 = CR
9.717 = CR

So our compression ratio is 9.717:1, which is not so hot for racing. What happens if you overbore the cylinders the standard .030 of an inch?

First you have to recalculate displacement:

4.030 x 4.030 x 3.48 x 0.7854 = 44.39 Cubic Inches

By swapping 44.39 into the equation with the rest of the figures staying the same (although any change made to the bore would also affect DC and G volumes), the compression ratio jumps to 9.848:1. The increase is because the piston is sweeping more volume as it moves up and down the cylinder. While the improvement is good, it isn't great.

Instead of over boring the cylinders for our hypothetical example, let's try increasing the piston pin height so that it is the same height as the deck at TDC. This means the deck clearance volume is 0, so you can leave it out of the equation:

(43.73 + 0.305 + 0.1885 + 4.272) /
(0.305 + 0.1885 + 4.272) = CR
10.18 = CR

By zeroing the deck the compression ratio jumps all the way up to 10.18:1, which is much better for racing. This change is more effective because any change you can make that reduces the volume of the combustion chamber at TDC (deck clearance volume, gasket volume, combustion chamber volume, minimizing the dish) has a far greater effect on the compression ratio.

This should mean two things to you: First, to make compression ratio changes without upsetting the rest of the engine package, look first at the cylinder heads. This is the area where you can have the greatest effect on compression ratio with the smallest effort. Second, if you have made a change to the cylinder heads, be sure to re-calculate the compression ratio using the new combustion chamber volume. This is especially important if you are polishing or otherwise changing the chambers, which makes them larger and lowers the compression. If you understand all of the variables, you can shave the head to bring the compression back to the range you need.

Jeff Dorton of Automotive Specialists demonstrates the proper process to use when cc'ing a combustion chamber. When doing this, make sure you have the valves and spark plugs you plan to use on hand, as these components can have an influence on chamber volume. Here, Dorton wipes a thin coat of grease on the valve to promote a good seal. If the valves are already installed on the head with the springs, this step isn't necessary.

Wipe a thin film of Vaseline or grease around the edges of the chamber.

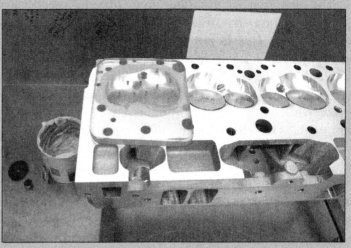

Volume checking kits use a clear piece of plastic that is placed over the chamber (the grease provides the seal). You can make the cover yourself; it just needs to have a smooth, flat surface with a couple of holes for filling the chamber with fluid and allowing the air to vent.

By using a marked burette, you can tell how many cc's of fluid were used to fill the combustion chamber. Be sure to note the volume of fluid in the burette before filling the combustion chamber.

Fill the combustion chamber with fluid completely. Mineral spirits or alcohol are better options than water. Be sure there are no air bubbles trapped against the clear plastic seal. Now, by using the increments marked on the burette determine how much fluid the chamber holds. Don't forget to convert to cubic inches if necessary.

Installing the Cam Bearings

The first step in installing any camshaft is properly installing the cam bearings. This is not difficult, but it does require a special cam installation tool. A cam installation tool uses a chuck to hold the bearing firmly while it is pressed into the cam bore. The chuck is normally wrapped with a thick rubber band to protect the bearing from scratches. A long bar extends from the chuck, allowing you to use a dead blow hammer to drive the bearing into position.

A cam-bearing installation tool is necessary because it is the only way to make sure that the cam bearings are installed perpendicular to the bore. The tool is a bit of an investment, but it is money well spent by the time you've built your second engine.

A cam bearing installation tool holds the cam bearing steady while it is driven into the housing bore. This tool is the only way to ensure the bearings are installed correctly in the housing bore without damage.

Installing the Cam

Installing the camshaft can get a little bit messy. Begin by lubricating the cam bearings with assembly lube. Beginning at the rear of the cam, lubricate it all the way up to the center cam journal. Use engine-assembly lubricant on the journals as well as the lobes if you are running a roller cam. If you are using a flat-tappet camshaft, lubricate the lobes with moly lube, which provides better protection against the sliding friction produced by the flat-tappet lifters. Use a moly lube or white-lithium paste on the cam's distributor gear.

Install the cam into the block, being extremely careful not to bang the edge of the cam journals or the lobes into the bearings or the housing bores. If you chip the edge of a lobe, the cam is ruined. Once the third journal is into the block, stop and finish lubricating the rest of the camshaft.

Do not forget the fuel pump eccentric. Now, finish installing the cam into the block. Before moving on, make sure the camshaft spins in its bores without binding.

Several companies offer "cam handles" which screw into the front of the cam and give you a nice, solid handle to hold on to. These are nice, but not absolutely necessary. One trick is to attach the cam timing gear loosely with a bolt or two, which can provide a better grip than trying to hold on to the very end of the camshaft.

Determining Pushrod Length

If you are used to working with stock Chevy small-blocks, finding the perfect pushrod length isn't as much of a priority as it is for a purpose-built race engine. That's because stock-style, non-roller rockers have a large flat that makes contact with the valvestem tip. Missing the pushrod length by a little bit isn't much of a problem because the flat on the rocker tip covers for the error.

Today, almost every racecar in every class can run roller-tip rocker arms. With the roller, the contact point between the rocker and the valvestem is very narrow. Miss the mark even by a little and you will get accelerated valveguide and valvestem wear. Big-lift camshafts and high-ratio rocker arms only exacerbate the problem. The pushrod length controls the location where the rocker tip contacts the valvestem, so getting that dimension correct is absolutely critical.

The problem with custom, hand-built engines is that it is almost impossible to predict the correct pushrod length before the engine is actually assembled. Factors that can

Loosely bolting the camshaft timing gear to the front of the cam can be a quick and easy way to get a better handle on the cam during installation. This is a roller cam that produces significantly less friction than a flat-tappet cam; only assembly lube is needed on the lobes.

On stud-mounted rocker systems, finding the correct pushrod length is critical because it determines where the rocker tip contacts the valvestem. In this example, the pushrod is slightly too short and the roller tip isn't centered over the valvestem.

affect pushrod length include, but aren't limited to:

- block deck height
- cylinder head deck height
- camshaft base circle
- lifter design and height
- valvestem length

Even the design of the rocker arms and their mounting system impacts pushrod length. Changing any one of these variables can require significant pushrod length changes, so it is often difficult to predict exactly what you will need ahead of time. Instead, the easiest and most reliable plan is to wait until the engine is assembled and then measure to see what length pushrods you will need. You can

then order them from your performance parts distributor and even have them overnighted to your location, if necessary.

Improperly sized pushrods in an engine equipped with roller-tipped rockers can be disastrous. When the valvetrain geometry is correct, the tip of the rocker makes contact with the top of the valvestem just north (the intake side) of the center of the valve tip. It then moves across the center of the valve tip at mid-lift, and to the exhaust side of the top at maximum lift, and then returns as the valve closes. The distance the roller tip travels on either side of the center should be equal. This maximizes the downward force the rocker places on the valve and minimizes side loading on the stem.

When the pushrod length is incorrect, the rocker arm tip won't be centered over the valvestem. In this case, when the camshaft activates the valvetrain, part of the force created by the motion of the rocker arm will be used to push the valvestem laterally as well as vertically. The valvestem then scrubs against the valveguide in the head, causing excessive wear on both components. This wear will open up the valveguides and allow the valve to flop around. If you are lucky, the only problems caused will be poor valve control (engine power will drop sooner at the higher RPM levels), a loss of compression, and an engine that mysteriously starts burning oil. If it isn't caught, however, it can lead to a broken valve head and even a junked engine.

Pro Tip: Controlling Cam Thrust

When the engine is running, resistance from the distributor gears act to push the camshaft toward the front of the block. In high-rpm racing applications this thrust can be significant, so a "cam button" is generally used to control camshaft thrust.

The button is simply a bearing attached to the end of the camshaft that presses against the timing cover to hold the cam in place. In severe applications, however, Dorton has seen the thin timing cover flex, causing problems.

To reduce the potential for problems, he uses a water pump drilled and tapped for a cam stop. A piece of threaded rod threads into the hole until it pushes against the timing cover. To provide additional support to the timing cover, Dorton prefers to weld a washer to the end of the threaded rod and then grind everything flat. This provides additional surface area for the cam button to press against. The cam stop is moved in or out until the cam

has between 0.008 and 0.010 of an inch of endplay, and then the assembly is locked into place with a locking nut and a little Loctite.

The cam stop simply screws into the water pump from the backside.

When running a steel cam—or in any high-rpm application, actually—a cam button is an excellent idea. Often, high-end timing sets are designed expressly to work with one.

The button usually works with a cam stop, which is a short length of threaded rod (bottom) to be run through a tapped hole in the water pump. It is used to support the front side of the timing cover. Dorton creates more surface area by welding a washer to the end of the rod and then grinding the face smooth (top).

Adjust the cam stop until the camshaft has between 0.008 and 0.010 of an inch of endplay.

Once endplay is correct, tighten the stop's location with a lock nut and a bit of Loctite.

Begin by covering the valvestem tip with ink from a Sharpie. This will be worn off wherever the rocker contacts it after just a few revolutions of the crank. You can also use machinist's dye.

With the lifter on the base circle of the cam, install either a pushrod you think is the best length or a checking pushrod (along with a lightweight checking spring) and the rocker arm. Adjust the rocker so that there is zero lash (or, if you are using a hydraulic lifter, tighten to the recommended preload). Now spin the motor over a few times by hand.

A checking pushrod, such as this one from Comp Cams, is made in two threaded sections that allow its length to be adjusted. You can expand or retract the pushrod until you find the correct length and then use that information to order the set you will use in the final assembly.

Remove the rocker and check the result. The line where the ink has been worn away shows where the rocker's roller tip has contacted the top of the valvestem. It should be centered, but here the line is a little too high. That means the pushrod is too short.

There are several ways of finding proper pushrod length, but when it comes to stud-mounted rocker systems, by far the simplest way is with a Sharpie and a wrench to turn the crankshaft. Begin by setting up the components for one cylinder. You can use an adjustable-length checking pushrod designed especially for this task.

Different manufacturers sell checking pushrods, but most operate on the same principle. They are typically a two-piece pushrod that is threaded to allow it to expand in length. You can adjust the checking pushrod's length until you have what you need, then use that as a guide to order the real set.

Some, such as Comp Cams' Hi-Tech Checking Pushrods are threaded so that each revolution is equal to 0.050 of an inch of length. The pushrod's collapsed length is marked, so after you find the correct size, simply count the number of revolutions the pushrod has been expanded and you will know the right size. Keep in mind, however, that a checking pushrod is significantly weaker than

After another try with a slightly longer pushrod, Dorton has the mark centered over the tip on the valve on the right.

a standard pushrod. A weaker checking spring must always be used with variable-length pushrods because standard racing valvesprings will bend them.

Whether you are using a checking pushrod or a standard piece that you think might fit correctly, begin by coloring the valve tip with either a Sharpie or machinist's dye. Then, install the pushrod and rocker arm in place while the lifter is on the base circle of the cam. If you are using a solid lifter, set the valvetrain to zero lash. If you are running a hydraulic lifter, tighten down the rocker adjuster to your normal preload.

Using a wrench on the nose of the crank, spin the motor over several times, then remove the rocker and check the mark left on the valve tip. The roller tip on the rocker should have left a shiny spot where it wore away the ink you placed on the valve tip.

If the pushrod length is correct, this mark should be centered across the top of the valvestem. If it is too

While adjusting your rockers to determine proper pushrod length, you should also verify that your rocker studs are the correct length. When the rocker arm is in the correct location you should be able to see most of the stud's threads for the adjuster nut. If the fulcrum covers too many threads, the lock nuts won't get good purchase on the stud and the system will be weakened.

All rocker designs are not the same—even if they are the same ratio. Both of these rockers have the same ratio, but the steel unit (right) has contact points that are farther outboard from the pivot point. If you are having problems with the rocker contacting the spring retainer when the valve is closed, you may need to consider changing your rocker design. On this engine, the aluminum rocker on the left was allowing the pushrod to contact the guideplates; the steel rocker fixed that.

high (closer to the lifter valley), try a slightly longer pushrod or lengthen the checker. If it is too low (closer to the exhaust ports), try a slightly shorter pushrod. Now simply repeat the process, adjusting the pushrod length each time, until you have the wear mark centered on the valve tip. Sometimes the low-tech methods really are the best.

If you are using a checking pushrod, you have two options for determining correct pushrod length. First, you can count the revolutions the pushrod has been expanded, calculate the extra length, and then add that to the pushrod's base length to find out what length pushrods you should order. Or, you can simply wrap a piece of tape around the threads so the length won't change, package the checking pushrod up, and send it off to your preferred pushrod manufacturer. They will match your checker against their stock and ship back to you the correct pushrods (along with your checker).

Attempting to measure the pushrod with a set of calipers is problematic because the oiling holes on either end make it difficult to find the true "tip" of the pushrod. Most manufacturers use a custom measurement tool that most of us don't have access to, so it's really better not to even try.

When you do receive your new pushrods, it's not a bad idea to repeat the checking process with the new rods. This is the easiest way to ensure a mistake hasn't been made and that you haven't been sent the wrong length pushrods. It's easy insurance.

Camshaft Timing

It's a common analogy to refer to the camshaft as the "brain" of the engine. And that's pretty accurate to think of the cam that way. After all, it's the camshaft that controls when the valves open, as well as how fast, how far, and for how long. If the events of the camshaft controls are not properly timed to piston position and spark timing, power will definitely suffer. The process of dialing in the cam's position relative to the crank is called "degreeing in" the cam, and its importance in building a racing engine cannot be overstated.

Often, the cam timing will be correct, and once you verify that you can move on. But if it isn't, you can use an adjustable timing set to move the cam's position forward or back to get results that match the specs provided by the camshaft's manufacturer.

Frequently, when cam timing is found to be incorrect, the manufacturer is immediately blamed for grinding the cam incorrectly. While this is a potential reason for incorrect cam timing, it's not the only one. More common reasons are a mistake made when machining the block or heads, extreme core shift, an incorrectly marked cam or crank gear for the timing chain, an incorrectly machined cam or crank gear keyway, or simply an accumulation of incorrect machining tolerances.

Even if everything is correct, there are times when you may want to purposely alter the cam timing, and being able to measure how much you've changed it is the only way to do it accurately. By advancing or retarding cam timing, you can influence where in the RPM range the engine makes power.

For most Chevy race engines, advancing the cam—or moving the point of maximum intake valve lift closer to TDC—will move the peak

Pro Tip: Pushrods and Shaft Mounted Rocker Systems

Shaft-mounted rocker-arm systems are becoming more common in racing and require a slightly different method for determining correct pushrod length. Instead of determining rocker arm height by sliding it up and down the rocker stud, a shaft-mounted system uses shims between the head and the base of the system.

Many manufacturers, such as T&D and Jesel, offer a simple tool or gauge that helps you know when the rocker pivot height is correct. After you do that, you simply use a checking pushrod to determine the distance between the pushrod cup in the rocker and the pushrod seat in the lifter (while the lifter is sitting on the base circle of the cam).

Also, Dorton recommends keeping the adjuster nut in the pushrod side of the rocker screwed in so that most of it is inside the body of the rocker. This is the strongest position, so when you determine the pushrod length, this is definitely where you want the adjuster.

Shaft-mounted rocker systems use shims to raise or lower the rocker arms in relation to the top of the valves. The bar is part of the checking tool to determine the correct height.

T&D Machine Products includes this gauge and the bar (mounted where the rockers would go) to determine the correct height. Add or remove shims until you can place one side of the checking tool on the bar and have the other side sit flush on the valve.

Once the shaft system is correctly shimmed, it is easy to find the correct pushrod length. You simply need to determine the distance between the pushrod cup in the rocker and the pushrod seat on the lifter when it is sitting on the base circle of the cam.

power lower in the RPM range. Retarding the cam, or going in the opposite direction, will move peak power higher in the RPM range.

Intake Centerline Method

Begin by installing your camshaft "straight up." This means the timing set should be indexed so that the marks on the cam and crank gears are pointing directly at each other.

The most commonly used method for degreeing in a cam is based around finding the intake centerline and then measuring everything based off of that. This method is popular because it doesn't require a lot of specialized equipment, it can be performed with the cylinder heads on or off of the engine (which does require a few different tools), it requires few complex calculations, and it is fairly straightforward.

The centerline method does, however, require a few specialized tools that you can either assemble yourself or purchase as a kit. In the illustrations here, I am using an on-head cam degreeing kit from Powerhouse Tools. As its name implies, this kit allows you to degree in a camshaft with the cylinder heads and valvetrain intact. It measures camshaft lift at the rocker arm, so if you want to determine lobe lift you must remember to divide out the rocker ratio. An on-head kit is useful if you will be performing camshaft swaps on an already-built engine.

A more standard cam degreeing kit works with the cylinder heads off. This type is typically more useful during engine assembly because the cam is normally degreed in as soon as the crankshaft, cam, and timing chain are in place. This style measures movement at the lifter so that you can see

actual lobe lift. With either style, the methods are virtually the same.

The first step is to make sure your camshaft and timing set are properly installed. It's okay if you have all of the valvetrain assembled, but it is better to degree the cam during the pre-fitting process so you can catch any potential problems early. Begin by installing the timing set "straight up," which is neither advanced nor retarded. The tick marks on the cam gear and crank gear should be pointed directly at each other. In other words, the cam gear tick mark should be pointing straight down while the tick mark on the crank gear points straight up.

You will notice in the photo illustrations that I am using an adjustable-length checking pushrod. When these photos were taken this engine was still in the pre-fitting stage, and I had not yet ordered the correct length pushrods. I am also using the lightweight checking springs included in the kit from Powerhouse.

If you choose to check the cam during the pre-fitting stages, just install one of the rocker arms you plan to run on the intake valve on the number-one cylinder. This is the second valve back on the right bank of cylinders. Use a checking pushrod at the proper length to set the valve at zero lash. If you are using a checking pushrod, make sure to always use a lightweight checking spring with it. Your race springs are too strong and will bend the checking pushrod. Finally, you should also have your cam card handy in order to check your findings against the manufacturer's specs.

Finding Piston TDC

Install your degree wheel on the nose of the crank and use a piece of

wire to form a pointer. You can mount the degree wheel by using the crank bolt, but this isn't the best idea because you will need to turn the crank both clockwise and counterclockwise. This can loosen the bolt and allow the wheel to slip. And anytime the degree wheel slips, it's time to start over.

The degree wheel can also usually be bolted directly to the harmonic damper, but the best method is to use a crank socket. This socket from Powerhouse not only secures the degree wheel but also allows you to use a ratchet with a 1/2-inch drive to easily turn the crank in either direction. Next, loop one end of the wire around a bolt and secure the wire to one of the cylinder heads. Bend it to form a pointer as close as possible to the wheel without touching it.

Now, remove the rocker arms (if installed) and install a piston stop through the spark-plug hole for the

Begin by installing your camshaft "straight up." This means the timing set should be indexed so that the marks on the cam and crank gears are pointing directly at each other.

number-one cylinder. There are many different versions of piston stops, but the only requirement is that it must physically stop the piston from reaching TDC without damaging anything. If you didn't remove the rocker arms earlier the valves could hit the piston stop before the piston does, giving you a false reading.

Slowly turn the crank until the top of the piston comes into contact with the piston stop. Spin the degree wheel (without turning the crank) to make this the zero point on your pointer, and tighten the wheel down. Now, turn the crank the opposite direction until the piston contacts the stop again. Make a note of, or mark the location of, the degree wheel indicated by the pointer with a pencil. Divide this number by two, giving you the piston TDC. For example, on this engine the point was 52 degrees. That means that the piston TDC is at the 26-degree mark.

Remove the piston stop and spin the crank until the pointer is at your TDC mark (26 degrees in this example). Without moving the crank, loosen the degree wheel and spin it

Piston stops take many forms but they all perform the same function—to provide some form of interference to keep the piston from reaching TDC without harming anything. This is the stop provided in the Powerhouse Products kit used in the demonstration photographs. It installs in the spark-plug hole and extends into the cylinder. When using a piston stop, rotate the crank slowly so the top of the piston makes gentle contact with the stop and doesn't bang into it.

until the zero mark is underneath the pointer. Now you know that piston's TDC for your checking cylinder is at zero degrees on your degree wheel.

Measuring Valve Movement

Now you are finally ready to get started. Go ahead and reinstall the rocker arms, setting the lash to zero. Mount the dial indicator on the head and position it so that it touches the outside edge of the intake valve retainer opposite the rocker. Make sure the indicator is parallel to the valvestem. If it isn't, your measurements will be incorrect.

Rotate the crankshaft clockwise until you reach the valve's maximum lift. You will know you have reached

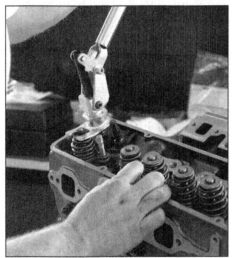

It is possible to degree a cam with the cylinder heads on and with the racing valvesprings in place, but it is much easier with a set of lightweight checking springs. Checking springs are mandatory if you are using an adjustable-length checking pushrod. To remove your valvesprings, you will need a spring compressor like this one from CV Products. It allows you to remove the valvesprings with the heads still on the engine, and it even works with the engine still in the racecar.

maximum lift when the pointer on the indicator begins to move back in the other direction. With the valve at max lift, set the dial indicator to zero.

Rotate the engine counterclockwise until the indicator reads 0.100 of an inch. Turning the crank clockwise again, turn the engine until the dial reads 0.050 of an inch. You always want to hit your points by spinning the crank in the same direction it will rotate when the engine is running. This will remove variables created by slack in the timing chain. If your rings provide a lot of friction, it can be easy to go too far. If this happens, back up and try again. Just do not set the dial to 0.050 of an inch by turning the crank counterclockwise.

Once you have the indicator on 0.050, record the degree-wheel reading. Continue to rotate the wheel until the indicator goes to 0.050 on the other side of maximum lift. Again, record the number the indicator is pointing to on the wheel.

You can find your point of maximum lift in terms of crank degrees by taking the two numbers and averaging them. In this example, I came up with 80 and 140 degrees on the wheel. The average is 110 degrees, which means the intake valve for the number-one cylinder achieves maximum lift 110 crank degrees after the piston has reached TDC. It is also exactly where the cam card provided for this camshaft says it should be. Repeat the process on the exhaust valve to find the exhaust lobe centerline.

Many engine builders like to check the crankshaft location at 0.050 of an inch of lobe lift to make sure the lobe's opening ramp is correct. When doing this with an on-head cam checker, remember that you are measuring valve lift and not just lobe lift. It can still be done, but you have to

Install the degree wheel on the crank and the wire to the engine with one end serving as a pointer. I prefer to use a crank socket with a screw-on nut that holds the degree wheel securely.

Mount the dial indicator on the head so it touches the outside edge of the valve retainer and reads the valve travel. To keep the geometry correct, the indicator must be parallel to the valvestem. Also, make sure the rocker arm does not touch the indicator at any point as the valve opens. This will throw off your readings.

When degreeing a camshaft with the cylinder heads off, you can measure the actual lobe lift at the lifter. This is usually done with a special dial indicator that actually fits inside the lifter bore and contacts the lifter face, or you can use a standard dial indicator to measure the movement of the lifter itself.

know that your valve lift is at 0.050 of an inch lobe lift. For example, if you are using 1.7:1 ratio rockers, then when the valve reaches 0.085 lift you know the lobe is at 0.050 of an inch. The equation is

Total Lift =
Lobe Lift x Rocker Ratio.

Piston-to-Valve Clearance

Now is also a great time to check your piston-to-valve clearances. With racing cams, we know that the intake valve is closest to the piston at 10

There are several options available if you need to either advance or retard the cam timing. One of the simplest, pictured here, is a cam degree bushing set. This one came from Comp Cams, but they are also available from other manufacturers. To use it, simply drill out the holes in the cam gear and press in the offset bushings.

degrees ATDC (after Top Dead Center). For the exhaust valve, the piston is closest to the valve at 10 degrees BTDC (before Top Dead Center). Though this can sometimes vary by a degree or two, it is usually safe to check piston-to-valve clearance at these two points.

To check intake valve clearance, turn the crank until the number-one piston is at 10 degrees ATDC. Position the dial indicator on the outside edge of the valve retainer with the checking spring in place, as described in the section on degreeing in a cam. Now, push the end of the rocker down until the valve comes in contact with the top of the piston. Check the total movement on the dial indicator.

Now measure exhaust valve clearance by turning the crank until the number-one piston is at 10 degrees BTDC and repeat the process. A good rule of thumb for a race motor is to always have at least 0.080 of an inch of clearance on the intake and 0.120 of an inch clearance on the exhaust. The exhaust requires more clearance because it is closing as the piston is coming up, and if the exhaust valve has lofted there is more potential for the piston to make contact.

STREET STOCK ENGINE BUILD

Many people say that auto racing is a rich man's sport, but that simply isn't true. The beauty of stock car racing is the great variety of classes available to choose from. You certainly can spend a ton of money racing if you want to, but there are racing classes that will allow you the thrill of door-to-door racing without requiring a liquid-cooled checkbook.

The typical entry-level class in stock car racing is called Strictly Stock or Street Stock. These cars are often Chevrolet Monte Carlos, Novas, or even Camaros. The rulebook, as the name suggests, almost always mandates stock or stock replacement parts. There are severe restrictions on how many and what types of race specific components are allowed. And as you might guess, this is especially true for the engine.

In this book I am detailing three separate engine builds for three distinctly separate racing classes. This chapter details a Street Stock-style engine built around the rules you typically see in this class. Street Stock almost always has the most restrictive rules, and they often vary from track to track.

The Street Stock engine is limited by the rulebook to mostly stock replacement components, but that doesn't mean you can't get an advantage on the competition by using smart engine-building techniques to maximize both power and durability.

Still, the general outline is that a stock block, cylinder heads, and crankshaft must be used. Connecting rods and the pistons may be aftermarket, but they must be stock replacement and cannot be forged. A racing oil pan is usually allowed. This is because a stock pan does not provide enough oil control, allowing centrifugal forces to push the oil away from the oil-pump pickup, which can lead to engine damage. Other common restrictions which limit power include maximum cam lift, minimum manifold vacuum pressure at idle, and a very small 350-cfm 2-barrel carburetor.

The good news about all these rules is building a competitive Street Stock motor for most racetracks can be done for between $3,500 and $5,000 if you are starting from scratch, and significantly less if you already have some parts on hand or don't mind digging around in a junkyard.

Building Street Stock racing engines is also a fun challenge because the secret to a winning engine is all about best assembly practices, not how much money you can spend on the latest racing widget. The bad news is you are forced to race with many engine components that were designed and manufactured with economy in mind rather than high performance or competition. You simply cannot bolt together a Street Stock engine like you would a rebuild for your pickup truck and expect it to work very well on the racetrack. The key to success is carefully modifying the stock components your rulebook requires so that they not only produce maximum power but can also withstand the rigors of high-rpm oval-track racing.

For this build, I enlisted the help of Ken Troutman and his staff at KT Engine Development in Concord, North Carolina. Ken and his brother Kevin lead KT Engines, which is unique because it regularly builds engines that span the motorsports spectrum. Its engines are run in everything from Mini-stocks to the Nextel Cup-based ARCA race series. When it comes to racing, KT Engines knows all the tricks and can translate many of the ideas that work well in high-end racing engines to the Street-Stock level.

The engine that I am building here is designed to fit within the most common Street Stock rules. Before beginning your own Street Stock engine project, you should first decide exactly where the engine and the car will be racing and get a copy of that track's rulebook. It is likely that your rulebook will differ in several minor points from the parameters I set up for our build. There may also be areas of your rulebook that are more lenient for you to take advantage of, as well as restrictions that would make portions of this build illegal. Regardless, the Street Stock class is a great place to begin your engine-building career.

The Block

The choices for your engine block are simple. Most rulebooks only allow an OEM (Original Equipment Manufacturers) stock block. For this build, I sourced a four-bolt stock block from General Motors Performance Parts. Ordering a new block from GMPP is more expensive than digging a Chevy 350 out of an old truck in a junkyard, but it also has a few advantages. First, when ordering a new block from GMPP you are assured that there aren't any hidden surprises like cracks or warpage from overheating. Other pitfalls of building with a used block include a block that is on its last legs from several rebuilds or even poor machine work from an engine rebuild shop at some point during the engine's earlier service life.

A new block arrives with all the stock dimensions intact, so you know exactly what you have to work with. New stock blocks from GMPP are available with four-bolt mains, but two-piece rear main seals are no longer available. For more information on converting a one-piece seal block to two-piece, see Chapter 2. If you are working with a block that has been removed from a passenger car, your best bet is to completely strip it and take it to an engine shop for a complete cleaning and inspection. This process includes baking the block to burn off water and lubricants and then bead blasting it to get rid of more stubborn carbon deposits and other debris. After that, the block should be inspected for problem areas and Magnafluxed to find any cracks. If it passes inspection, you can have your engine builder complete any necessary machining processes, including honing the cylinders, line honing the main bores, and decking the block.

For some of these processes, such as decking the block, some pre-fitting is required. You may need to take the block back to your shop after cleaning and inspection. Once there, pre-fit the rotating assembly with your crank and one rod and piston so that you can measure how much the block will need to be decked. After the machining is complete, you can have the block cleaned if that facility has a mechanical washer, or you can take the block home and clean it yourself. Be sure to keep a thin coat of WD-40 or some other type of lubricant on any freshly machined surfaces to prevent corrosion.

Rotating Assembly

Here is one area where you generally have a little more leeway. Rules require stock replacement rods and pistons, but it is possible to stay within the rules and make some real improvements in the area of the rotating assembly.

Speed Pro produces several pistons that qualify as stock replacements. They are hypereutectic, which means they are still a casting, but with high silicon content that makes them stronger than stock castings. You can get them with either four-piston pocket "eyebrows" like stock Chevy pistons or with only two-piston pockets. The pistons are also available with or without a friction-reducing coating on the skirts. Finally, some pistons also are available with a floating wristpin. For this build, I chose a hypereutectic piston with the coating on the skirts and floating pins.

Chevrolet's stock pistons have four valve reliefs, so that the pistons can go into the engine in either direction. By using pistons that have only two valve pockets, I planned to increase the compression ratio a couple of points. But upon further inspection of the pistons, I realized that this piece uses the same slug as the piston with four valve pockets. This means it has extra material under the piston top, into which the pockets can be cut. Because of this, these pistons are approximately 40 grams heavier

than the pistons with the stock-style four-valve pockets. If your rules allow either piston style, you have a choice between a little higher compression ratio or a lighter-weight rotating assembly. The pros and cons of either choice probably balance out in terms of final engine performance.

For connecting rods, I went with a relatively new company called K1 Technologies. K1 specializes in producing cost-effective performance rods. Although it is a new company, K1 is a division of Carrillo, which has a fantastic reputation in the racing industry. K1 offers a stock-appearing forged rod, which has several advantages over an actual stock unit. The rods arrive pre-balanced and utilize cap screws, which are significantly stronger than press-in rod bolts and nuts. The cap screw design is lighter because the nuts are eliminated. It also produces a stronger and more stable connecting rod.

Generally, a stock cast crank, while certainly not as strong as a forging, can reliably handle 400 hp. Exercise caution when using a refurbished crank. In order to bring a used crank back to usable status, the rod and main journals are sometimes turned down 0.010 to 0.030 of an inch. The smaller journal size can be made up with thicker bearings, but the reduced diameter of the journals reduces the crank's strength. The crank is bone stock and retains the stock 2.100 rod journal size and 3.480 stroke.

Cylinder Heads and Valvetrain

Almost all rulebooks require stock cylinder heads. This is the

area of the engine that requires the most work to make the stock components usable for racing. If your rulebook doesn't specify, the best choices are GM Vortec heads. If those aren't allowed, try to source a pair of the venerable "Double Hump" cylinder heads. The stamp that looks like two camel humps on the ends of the heads easily distinguishes these. Double Humps are becoming scarce however, and most tracks are outlawing them. You most likely will have to go with a set of standard 23-degree Chevy heads, which was our choice for this build. Our heads are also used, which is what most engine builders will have to begin with.

Since valve sizes cannot be modified, it makes sense to save a few bucks by reusing the stock valves. More modern valvespring designs can help performance considerably. Newer GM LS1 engines use beehive-shaped valvesprings that start out at a standard diameter but have a progressively smaller diameter towards the top of the spring. This lightens the spring and also allows a considerably smaller and lighter retainer. Since most rulebooks require stock-style components, these springs can be legally installed on a 23-degree cylinder head.

Comp Cams is currently leading the way in producing high-quality beehive springs and retainers for racing use. The drawback with these springs is that they cannot be double nested, so they do not work well with very aggressive solid cams. But since Street Stock rules mandate hydraulic cams with limited lift, they are absolutely perfect for this application.

Ignition

Another quirk of Street Stock-level racing is that stock-style ignitions are required. In the 1970s and '80s Chevy engines used an HEI ignition. HEI stands for "high energy ignition," and the units are notable because they are entirely self-contained within the distributor. There is no external coil.

While the HEI is a good design due to its simplicity and durability, it isn't designed to meet the needs of the stock car racer. Even in a stock low-compression engine, a stock HEI cannot produce enough spark to reliably fire all eight cylinders after about 5,000 rpm. Increasing the compression makes the problem even worse.

Because of this, several ignition companies produce HEI upgrade kits. Since most Street Stock rules will not allow an external coil or control box,

HEI upgrades generally center around a new high-power internal coil and a more efficient module—which essentially is the brain of the unit. Most upgrade kits are relatively easy to install and work well.

The route I chose, however, was to install a brand new performance HEI ignition from Performance Distributors. Performance Distributors specializes in HEI ignitions and will custom-build units for racers. I have previously tested these units and found they can reliably fire a race engine well beyond 8,000 rpm, which is more than a Street Stock will ever see. This is an advantage because the extra power produced by this ignition allows you to open up the plug gaps and still get a reliable spark. A wider plug gap helps produce more efficient combustion in the chambers, which is especially useful in this engine because the stock cylinder heads are not nearly

as efficient as modern designs. The Performance Distributors ignition can also be built with custom advance curves best suited to meet your specific engine's needs.

Even if your block is new, it's a good idea to have the cylinders honed for a few reasons. First, most rulebooks allow you to bore the cylinders 0.030 of an inch oversized, and it's always a good idea to take advantage of all the displacement you can get. Second, stock blocks are not honed with a deck plate in place. Torquing the cylinder heads on the deck will distort the cylinder bores, so a race engine should always be honed with a deck plate in place to mimic the distortion caused by the heads.

Rules disallow forged pistons but do allow hypereutectic pistons, which are considerably stronger than stock cast units. Hypereutectic simply means these pistons have a higher silicon level than most aluminum castings. One effect of the increased silicon is to limit heat expansion, so piston-to-bore clearance should be considerably tighter. Where a forged race piston may require 0.006 to 0.009 of an inch between the piston and cylinder wall, a hypereutectic typically needs only 0.003 of an inch. Be sure your machinist knows exactly what pistons you are using before honing your block.

Before decking the block, engine builder Ken Troutman mocks up the number-one cylinder with the piston and rod (complete with bearings). The crank is held in place by the two outer main caps and bearings. The piston was found to be 0.028 of an inch below the deck at TDC. Measure piston depth at TDC at all four corners of the block (cylinders 1, 2, 7, and 8) so that you can tell if the deck of the block slopes from one end to the other.

The piston depth at all four corners must be determined before the block can be properly decked. Approximately 0.022 of an inch was cut off the decks of this engine to achieve a piston depth of 0.006 of an inch at TDC.

Although it isn't great, oil dripping onto the camshaft through the valley tray absorbs kinetic energy and is a drain on horsepower. There is enough oil dripping through the bottom of the lifter galleries to properly lubricate the cam, so Kevin Troutman taps the drain holes in the center of the lifter valley for plugs to be inserted later. When tapping these holes, be sure not to tap all the way through. Without a hard stop, the set screw plugs could extend too far and potentially make contact with the camshaft. Do not install any set screws until all the machining processes are completed and the block has been thoroughly cleaned.

Now is also a good time to tap the holes in the oil galleries in order to replace the press-in plugs with set screws. As noted before, do not install any set screws until all the machining processes are completed and the block has been thoroughly cleaned.

Here's a better shot of the reworked oil drain holes in the front of the block. These also feed lubrication to the timing chain. All three oil galleries above the cam tunnel should be tapped for set screw plugs.

Since oil drain-back from the cylinder heads is limited in the valley tray, use a grinder to open up the drain holes in the front and rear of the block. In stock blocks, casting flash can obstruct a large portion of these drain holes.

One of the nice things about using an aftermarket performance crank is that the journal sizes are very consistent. That is often not the case when you are forced to race with a stock cast crank. Stock Chevy cranks are often a few tenths of a thousandth smaller at the fifth main journal. This is acceptable in stock form, but bad news in a race engine. Main bearing clearance should be held between 0.0022 and 0.0025 of an inch. On this build the first four main journals required mixing one standard-sized bearing shell with one shell that was 0.001 of an inch undersized. The fifth main, which is the thrust bearing, required two undersized shells.

After the block was cleaned, 1/2-inch-wide set screws with #13 thread pitch were installed in the valley tray with red Loctite on the threads.

Ken Troutman prefers to use heavy engine assembly grease on the main bearings for extra protection during startup. Before installing the crank, squirt a little motor oil into each of the oil galleries that feed the main journals until you see the oil dripping into the cam journal on the other side of the gallery. This helps ensure there is no trash plugging any of the galleries.

Before installing the crank, lubricate your camshaft and install it in the block. With the crank out of the way, it's a lot easier to see what you are doing, and you can also reach inside the block to help guide the cam in place. This reduces the chance of chipping either a cam bearing or a lobe.

As you can see from the holes in the counterweight, this crank had to be extensively rebalanced for the lighter-weight rods and pistons. On a higher-end race engine, Troutman would grind down the counterweights and install small amounts of heavy metal to achieve balance. This approach isn't cost effective in a Street Stock motor where many tracks have claimer rules for as little as $750. Instead, the more traditional method of drilling lightening holes is used at the cost of a little more windage.

Kevin Troutman checks crankshaft endplay. He began with all the main caps torqued in place, but crankshaft endplay was only 0.002 of an inch instead of the recommended 0.004 to 0.007 of an inch. The next step, shown here, was to remove all the caps and check play against just the upper shells. Endplay was still insufficient.

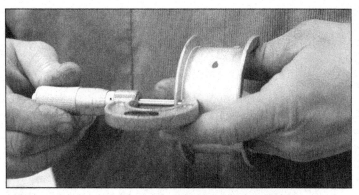

The culprit was found to be the fifth main bearing. Portions of the thrust face were too thick.

The standard timing chain set was switched out for an adjustable billet unit from Comp Cams. The double chain, however, rubbed the block and required a little grinding. It is often difficult to tell exactly how much must be ground around the oil gallery bosses until the timing set is bolted up. If this is discovered after the block has already been cleaned, just make sure to tape everything up thoroughly prior to grinding.

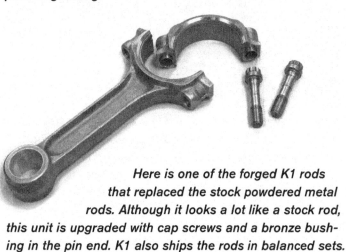

Here is one of the forged K1 rods that replaced the stock powdered metal rods. Although it looks a lot like a stock rod, this unit is upgraded with cap screws and a bronze bushing in the pin end. K1 also ships the rods in balanced sets.

The bearing was brought into spec by lightly rubbing the thrust faces against #040 sandpaper. Wet the paper with solvent and use a flat block to remove a small amount of material. This is a good solution anytime you need a couple thousandths more crankshaft endplay. Just be cautious and rub the thrust face very lightly.

This billet timing set from Comp Cams offers much improved durability over the stock unit and allows easy cam timing adjustments with multiple keyways on the crank gear.

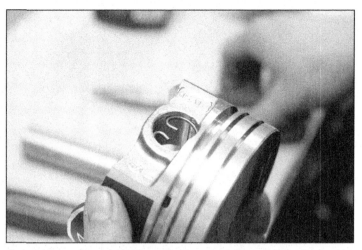

The Speed Pro pistons that will be matched with the rods use a friction-fighting coating on the skirts to reduce drag. The coating also helps eliminate scuffing of the cylinder walls, which is important for use in a stock block because the iron is normally much softer than you will find in a Bow Tie block.

Speed Pro offers stock replacement pistons either in a press-fit pin configuration or with floating wristpins. If you are allowed, you should always choose the floating pin option because it reduces the chance of the wristpin galling in the piston pin bore. Instead of spiral locks, this piston uses snap wire locks, which are easily installed with a pair of needle-nose pliers.

The piston pin relies on splash oiling for lubrication. This is limited at engine startup though, so be sure to liberally apply engine assembly lube to both the piston pin bore and the small end of the connecting rod.

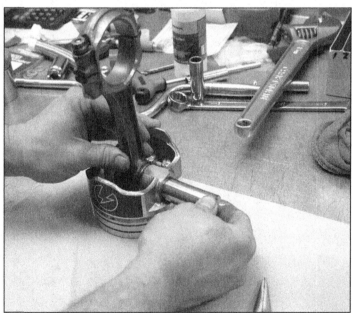

Hold the connecting rod in position and slide the wristpin into place.

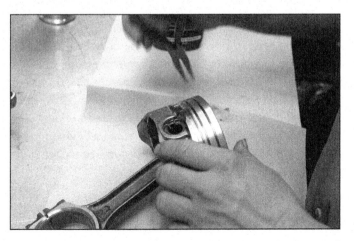

Using a pair of needle-nose pliers, squeeze the lock ring and insert it into the pin bore. Then use the end of the pliers to pop the ring into its groove inside the bore.

Don't forget to check the ring's radial depth. When inserted as shown here, the entire width of the ring should be able to fit inside the piston's ring land.

When checking piston ring gap, it is critical that the ring is square in the cylinder bore. You can do this using an old piston with a ring in the second ring land. Insert the piston upside down into the bore and push down on the new ring until the ring installed in the old piston contacts the deck of the block.

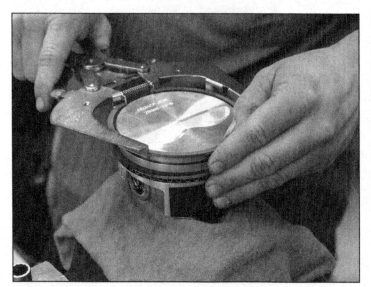

When done properly, you will have the caps of the connecting rods off several times while checking bearing clearances. A lightweight impact wrench like this one from Ingersoll Rand makes bolt removal a lot easier and quicker. It is also useful for many other areas on an engine. However, don't make the mistake of thinking you can use a power tool to replace a torque wrench when it comes to fastening nuts and bolts.

Standard width rings, like I was forced to use in this Street Stock build, can be difficult to install on a piston. A ring expander tool can reduce a lot of frustration and pinched fingers when installing a set of rings. You simply use it to expand the ring and slide it over the piston.

The K1 rods came equipped with nice 3/8-inch ARP rod bolts. After lubricating the threads with extreme pressure lube, 52 ft-lbs of torque consistently gave the correct 0.006 of an inch of bolt stretch.

Kevin Troutman degrees in the cam. Most Street Stock rules require a cam with near-stock lobe lift. It also must be able to pull around 17 inches of vacuum at idle speed. Generally, this limits duration and overlap, and it requires much milder grinds than you would normally see on a racing cam. Comp Cams spec'd a camshaft with 238 degrees of duration on the intake and 242 on the exhaust with 0.283 of an inch lobe lift and 110 degrees of lobe separation. The intake centerline was ground at 106 degrees. Street Stock racing is all about acceleration out of the corners, so Ken Troutman recommended advancing the cam two degrees to increase low end torque. This is achieved on this timing set by rotating the crank gear to the keyway marked "A2."

While you can squeeze a feeler gauge between the rods to measure connecting rod side clearance, a more accurate method is to use a dial indicator on a magnetic base. Rod clearance on a stock crank will often be on the high side because a stock crank has very little fillet. The 0.019 of an inch of clearance found here was well within tolerance.

A stock, standard-pressure oil pump works well in this application. Don't make the mistake of using a high-volume oil pump because it is overkill and drains horsepower. One upgrade you will need to make is to ditch the stock oil pump driveshaft with its plastic collar (on left). The collar, which connects the shaft to the pump, is the weak link, and if it breaks you will lose oil pressure immediately. Instead, invest in a performance pump shaft like this one from ARP, which uses a steel engagement collar.

Troutman checks oil pump pickup depth compared to a measurement from the oil pan. I had almost 3/4 of an inch of clearance between the bottom of the pickup and the pan because the pickup was designed to work with a high-volume pump, which is thicker. The correct gap is between 1/4 and 3/8 of an inch.

Bending the tube in a vise and then adding a few washers under the mounting flange adjusts the depth of the oil pump pickup. You can seal the pickup tube in the pump housing with green Loctite so that it doesn't draw air.

This Fel-Pro one-piece oil pan gasket is seen more in hot rodding than racing but works well in this application. Remember to put a dab of silicone at the edges of the front and rear rails.

After installing the harmonic damper, check the accuracy of the timing pointer. Find TDC of the number-one piston with a dial indicator and make sure the timing pointer is set to zero. If not, adjust the pointer to ensure that your timing light is correct later on. Being off by a degree or two here can spell the difference between maximum power and a detonating engine.

If you are using in a sheet-metal pointer like this one, try squirting silicone between the back of the pointer and the timing cover. This will help ensure that the pointer doesn't get bent later and throw off your timing readings.

Stock Chevrolet heads use press-in rocker studs that will loosen if used with high-rate racing valvesprings. They must be pulled with a stud extractor and replaced with screw-in rocker studs.

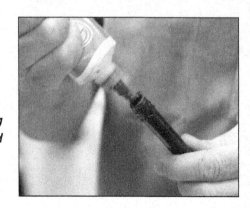

Ditch your stock fuel pump pushrod for a lightweight performance piece to reduce fuel pressure flutter at high RPMs. A dab of extreme pressure lube at both ends of the pushrod will protect the cam and fuel pump during startup and will also hold the pushrod in place inside the engine while you bolt up the fuel pump.

Before investing a lot of time upgrading a set of stock cylinder heads, it's always a good idea to have them checked out. Here, Nathan Allmond magnetizes the head and dusts it with iron filings, which will cling to any cracks and make them easy to see.

These heads had not seen a ton of miles so the valves can be reused after touching up the seats, which will save a little money. In the center is a valve as it came out of the head, and surrounding it are valves from the same head that have been bead blasted.

One trick to aid flow into the combustion chambers in an engine with limited valve lift is to back-cut the valves. This puts a 30-degree angle above the 45-degree seat, which removes some obstruction to the air/fuel mixture as it moves past the valve.

Kevin Troutman gives the heads the standard three-angle valve job. He also ensures that all the seats are at the same height in the head so that the pushrod length and rocker arm geometry are consistent. This is key to making the valvetrain work efficiently, race after race. With the right selection of cutters, a good cylinder head man can also significantly clean up the throat of the port legally to improve airflow.

On the other side of the head, the valveguides are cut to accept race-grade valve seals, which will provide better oil control. The press-in rocker stud bosses are also cut down and tapped in preparation for the Crane Cams 7/16-inch screw-in studs.

I decked the heads to 64 cc's, which is in line with most rulebooks. You can see that this is pretty significant as it reached into the intake valve area and also cut into the spark plug boss. Along with the 4.030-inch bore, 3.48-inch stroke, and 0.028 of an inch thick head gasket, this creates a 10.2:1 compression ratio.

Cam options are limited to pretty mild lobe grinds. You can consider this an opportunity to take advantage of spring combinations that wouldn't work in more powerful race motors. These Comp Cams beehive springs and small retainers weigh significantly less than a conventional double-nested valvespring. They maintain good control at an installed height of 1.73 inches with 120 lbs of pressure on the seat and 285 lbs at full lift.

The easiest way to make power is to maximize engine compression, and the most efficient way to do that is by minimizing the size of the combustion chambers. To determine your head's chamber volume, you need a cc kit. The stock Chevy heads started out at 78 cc's.

Combined with the 1.6:1 ratio rocker arms, the 0.283 lift lobes create total valve lift of 0.453 of an inch. That's enough to require the pushrod holes to be elongated slightly with a grinder.

Rules require hydraulic flat-tappet lifters, but you should avoid stock units, which aren't able to cope with long stretches of high RPMs. The stock lifters will "pump up" or basically go solid at maximum extension, which can keep the valves from closing. These performance lifters from Comp Cams feature more consistent crowns on the lobe faces and resist over pumping with oil. Before installation the faces of the lifters are coated with Comp's camshaft break-in lube.

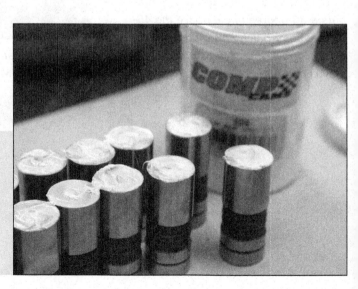

After coating the lifter bores with motor oil, insert the lifters in their bores.

Don't forget to plug the dipstick holes on either side of the block. Silicone works well here and is easy to remove if you ever wish to return the block to over-the-road duty.

Use a thin composite head gasket to help keep compression up. This Victor Reinz head gasket measures 0.028 of an inch compressed.

ARP 7/16-inch head bolts provide good clamping load to seal the cylinder heads. Several of the head bolts and rocker studs on a Chevrolet thread into water jackets. To avoid leaks, make sure to coat all the threads with Teflon thread sealer.

Rules require stock-style stamped steel rocker arms, which have a ratio of 1.5:1. Crane Cams, however, sells a set of stock-appearing stamped rockers in 1.6:1 ratio that bear no markings to give away their slightly higher ratio. Technically, they aren't legal at most tracks, but you can bet you will be racing plenty of cars equipped with them on the track.

The stamped rocker arms use a fulcrum ball to control the pivot point. Regardless of the manufacturer you use, these steel fulcrums are the weak point of this design. Be sure to liberally coat the contact point of the fulcrum ball with a thick lubricant like extreme pressure lube.

Pushrods are a stock length set from Speed Pro. Since we've switched to guideplates, hardened pushrods are required. Tightening the rocker lock (with the lifter on the cam's base circle) until there is no slack between the rocker arm, pushrod, and lifter sets the lash. You can tell this by spinning the pushrod while tightening the lock nut until you feel tension on the pushrod. Then tighten the lock nut an additional quarter-turn.

Check piston-to-valve clearance by installing lightweight checking springs on the intake and exhaust valves for the number-one cylinder. Use a dial indicator to measure movement of the retainer and, with the timing pointer at 10 degrees ATDC, measure the distance you can move the rocker and valve by hand until the valve contacts the top of the piston. Do the same thing with the exhaust valve at 10 degrees BTDC. Because this is a hydraulic system, minimum piston-to-valve clearance should be a little larger than solid-roller systems with at least 0.100 of an inch for the intake and 0.120 of an inch for the exhaust valves.

Some classes allow a Late Model Stock-style Edelbrock dual-plane intake manifold, which is being installed here. Others may require a stock intake. If you can, avoid the cast iron stock intake at all costs because it doesn't perform nearly as well and weighs a ton.

The stock cylinder heads have an exhaust gas recirculation port that routes hot exhaust gasses back into the intake. Racecars don't use EGR valves, so the easiest way to take care of this is to plug the hole for the EGR valve in the top of the intake. However, this allows exhaust gasses to unnecessarily heat the air/fuel mixture inside the manifold, which harms horsepower. Instead, cut a piece of sheet metal to plug the hole in the cylinder head and then seal it with plenty of high-temp silicone.

If you try to run a stock HEI in a high-compression Street Stock engine you are virtually guaranteed to suffer from a high-speed miss at 5,000 rpm and beyond. A Performance Distributors HEI ignition qualifies in most rulebooks and can provide plenty of power to the spark plugs well beyond 8,000 rpm. If an aftermarket unit isn't allowed, try an internal upgrade kit for a stock HEI. Also, Performance Distributors sells its high-power unit with a black cap and no markings, making it very difficult to differentiate from a stock unit.

The Spec Sheet

Engine: ....Street Stock
Displacement: ....355 ci
Bore: 4.030
Stroke: 3.480
Compression ratio: 10.2:1

Short Block
Crankshaft: ....Stock cast iron
Main journals: 2.45
Main bearing clearance: ....0.0022 – 0.0025 in
Rod journals: 2.100
Rod bearing clearance: ....0.0020 – 0.0025 in
Connecting Rods: ....Forged I-beam
Rod length: 5.700
Pin size: 927
Rod bolt size: 3/8
Pistons: ....Hypereutectic aluminum flat top
Rings: ....5/64, 5/64 & 3/16 in
Deck Height: 9.006
Piston compression distance: 1.560
Piston height: ....0.006 in hole
Oiling: ....Wet sump

Cylinder Head
Head: ....Stock cast iron
Intake valve: 1.940
Exhaust valve: 1.500
Combustion Chamber: ....64 cc
Head bolts: 7/16

Valvetrain
Camshaft: ....Cast
Lifters: ....Hydraulic flat tappet, 0.843 diameter
Pushrods: ....5/16 diameter, 0.060 wall
Rockers: 1.6:1
Valve lift: ....0.453 in
Lobe lift: ....0.283 in
Duration: ....238 intake, 242 exhaust @ 0.050
Valve Lash: ....Hydraulic

Ignition
Ignition: ....HEI
Firing order: ....Standard
Plug gap: ....0.035 in

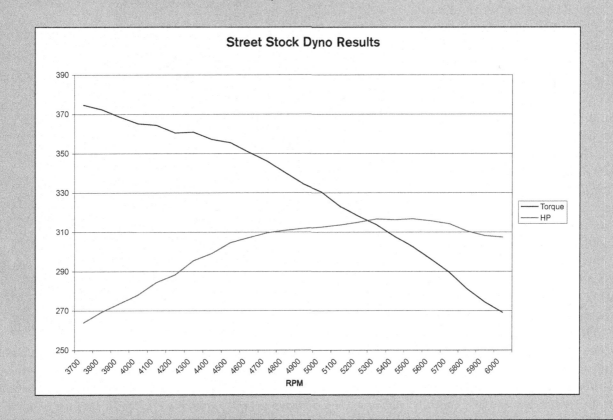

Street Stock Dyno Results

NASCAR LATE MODEL STOCK ENGINE BUILD

The NASCAR Late Model Stock class is one of the most popular in NASCAR's Weekly Racing Series. Because of that, the Late Model Stock engine rules are copied for many other classes by other sanctioning bodies. The defining feature of this class is the 2-barrel, 500-cfm carburetor limit; it affects everything else in the build.

This carburetor rule is popular because it is an effective way to limit engine power. Since the carburetor sits on top of the engine, it is easy to access for tech inspection. At race speeds, the 500-cfm 2-barrel severely restricts the amount of air the pistons can pull into the engine on the induction stroke. The effect is that the carburetor functions as a restrictor plate.

Incidentally, you cannot compare cfm's between 2-barrel and 4-barrel carburetors. Although the cfm numbers are close, a 650-cfm 4-barrel can actually flow much more air than a 500-cfm 2-barrel; even more than the 30-percent rating increase would suggest.

Although there are other rules controlling what you can and cannot

A NASCAR Late Model Stock-level engine can be a challenge to build well, because the 2-barrel carburetor required by the rules poses a significant restriction to airflow. Smart engine builders gain an advantage in this class by concentrating on ways to limit horsepower losses inside the engine.

do in the engine, the restrictive carburetor affects just about every other component choice in the build. Limiting the available airflow restricts the engine to around 6,500 rpm and somewhere around the 400-hp range. Because of this, the smart engine builder concentrates on lightening components inside the engine and making sure every part functions with as little drag as possible. Essentially, building a Late Model Stock-style engine is as much about building an ultra-low drag engine as it is about building big HP.

Keith Dorton, the owner and lead engine builder of Automotive Specialists, is the resource for our NASCAR Late Model Stock engine build. Dorton is the most successful engine builder in the history of the USAR Hooters Pro Cup Series. His engines have powered the champions in all but one year since the series began in 1997. Although quite a bit more powerful than a NASCAR Late Model Stock engine at approximately 650 horsepower, a Pro Cup motor is also restricted and utilizes many of the same tricks. Dorton also built the winning engine for the 1990 Daytona 500, the ultimate restrictor-plate race.

The Block

Besides the carburetor rule, most other rules in Late Model Stock racing are designed to hold costs in check. For example, most rulebooks require a stock Chevy block or a sportsman block available from GMPP. Dorton says he has no problem using a good stock block because, with the addition of four bolt main caps, they are more than capable of withstanding the power levels these engines produce. If you come across a stock block with two-bolt mains, it is easy to upgrade the block with an aftermarket four-bolt main cap kit.

Dorton says that for this class a stock block is actually preferable over a Bow Tie block, even when the rules allow it, because the Bow Tie is reinforced with extra material in several areas. This makes the block stronger and capable of withstanding Nextel Cup power levels, but it also makes the block several pounds heavier, and the extra strength isn't necessary for this engine package.

Also, since the rules require stock blocks, no aluminum is allowed. Even if your rules don't say anything specifically, stay away from blocks out of tuned port injection engines because they are quite a bit different. Other than an upgrade to four-bolt main caps made from steel, the only other significant change is to switch the rear main seal to a two-piece unit if necessary.

If you are using a stock block that has seen service in an over-the-road car, make sure to have the cylinder bores sonic checked. You want the thrust side of the cylinder (the side of the cylinder bore the crank is rotating toward) to be at least 0.120 of an inch thick. Maximum cylinder overbore is usually limited to around 0.060 of an inch.

Rotating Assembly

Most rulebooks stipulate a minimum crankshaft weight of around 49 lbs, but usually do allow an aftermarket forged steel unit. This should be considered a must, since a stock cast crank will quickly crack and break in this engine package. The forged material is not only stronger, but a performance crank is also usually constructed with a nice radius on the journal fillets, which adds strength. Tricks like knife edging the leading edge of the counterweights are almost always outlawed, but when it is legal it is definitely helpful in reducing windage. The stock 3.5-inch stroke also cannot be changed, although the rod journal size is sometimes allowed to be smaller than the stock 2.100-inch journal size.

Since the horsepower is not outrageous, the rods and pistons used are some of the lightest you will find anywhere in racing. Dorton uses rods shaved down to 456 grams each, which is approximately 100 grams less than a standard rod. The rod, manufactured by Carrillo in this case, is designed specifically for this style of racing.

The pistons also are significantly lighter than what you would see in most other applications. They use inboard pin bosses to shorten the wristpins to cut weight, and they also get by with a minimal slipper skirt design. A coating on the small skirts helps prevent scuffing the cylinder walls.

Flat-top pistons are also a common requirement in this level of racing. Along with a minimum combustion chamber rule, it helps limit compression to hold horsepower down. It is not allowed to set pistons up so that they extend out of the deck of the block at TDC. It is a good idea to choose a piston with a ring land that is close to the piston top because it helps maintain compression. Another helpful idea is to use the thinnest head gasket possible, which will also help maximize compression.

Cylinder Heads and Valvetrain

Again, the rulebook is the prime motivator when it comes to cylinder head choices. Only cast iron, direct-replacement heads produced by General Motors are all allowed. GMPP does, however, offer a Bow Tie 23-degree cylinder head that is cast iron with straight plugs and fits the rulebook. This is another component produced specifically for Late Model Stock-level racing and it is significantly better than a stock 23-degree cylinder head. Because of this, your only reasonable choice is to go with the cast iron Bow Tie heads.

Other rules governing the heads and valvetrain include a requirement that all valves be stainless steel with the stock stem diameter. Maximum valve sizes are 2.020 inches for the intakes and 1.600 inches for the exhausts, and the valve job is limited to three angles. No hand or machine work is permitted above the bottom of the valveguide. Finally, titanium retainers are usually allowed, but shaft-mount rocker arms are not.

Oiling

Late Model Stock-level rules all require wet-sump oiling, meaning the reserve engine oil is held in the oil pan below the crank. An internal oil pump driven off of the distributor shaft is usually also required, but sometimes a belt-driven, external single-stage pump is allowed. When an external pump is allowed, that is definitely the way to go. This is because it creates extra room inside the oil pan and allows better control over oil pressure at speed.

Because limiting horsepower losses in this class is a major concern, oil pan design is critical. Windage from oil contacting the rotating crankshaft is one of the biggest causes of horsepower loss inside the engine, so keeping oil in the bottom of the pan and away from the crankshaft is very important. This also becomes difficult in a stock car, because you want the engine as low in the chassis as possible to maximize handling by keeping the center of gravity low. A very deep oil pan simply isn't an option, so instead kick outs on both sides of the pan are used along with a windage tray. A good oil pan will also have gated dams to encourage oil to flow toward the pickup and then hold it there.

Typically, most Late Model Stock engine builds begin with a stock block that spent the first part of its life inside a truck or older passenger car. This is an old truck block with its original four-bolt nodular-iron main caps.

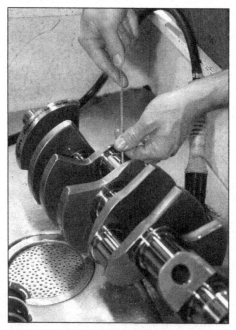

If an aftermarket forged steel crank is allowed, you should definitely take advantage of it. In addition to being stronger than a cast crank, a good forged crank will be designed for a lighter piston and rod combination and will be easier to balance. Rod and main journal diameters are also typically more consistent.

The use of studs rather than bolts for the main caps puts less stress on the threads inside the block. If you are using an older block and you suspect the threads are not in like-new condition, the use of studs is a great idea. Also, make sure to use a lubricant on the threads when torquing the main caps. Bolt manufacturers will often provide different torque numbers whether you use motor oil or extreme pressure lube.

Don't wait until final assembly to test fit your rear main seal. With both halves of the seal in place, make sure the lips of both halves of the seal match up correctly at the parting lines. Dorton says that occasionally the two halves of the seal will be slightly different, which will result in an oil leak.

Before placing the main seal in place for the final time, Dorton adds a thin film of gasket sealer to the lip it seats on.

Dorton prefers to use coated bearings for an extra bit of insurance against a spun bearing caused by a loss of oil pressure. The main journal size is 2.45 inches and bearing clearance is held between 0.0022 and 0.0025 of an inch.

This block was produced sometime after 1986 and required a conversion to a two-piece main seal (the aluminum piece in the bottom of the photo).

To reduce the chances of an oil leak, make sure the seal's parting lines are not aligned with the parting lines of the seal retainer.

Finally, prep the main bearings with a liberal coating of assembly lube and the lip of the main seal with a light coat of motor oil.

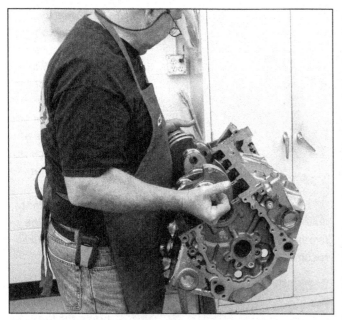

The crankshaft is now ready to be lowered into position.

The caps are put into position, and with extreme pressure lube on the threads, the 7/16 main studs are torqued to 70 ft-lbs in two equal steps.

It can be difficult to move the crankshaft enough to measure endplay using just your fingers, so try using screwdrivers between the side of the main caps and the crank's counterweights (just stay away from the thrust bearing). Endplay should be between 0.005 and 0.010 of an inch.

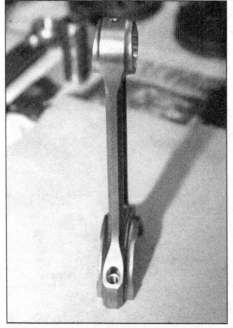

Dorton uses these connecting rods from Carrillo designed for low-horsepower race engines. They are a modified I-beam style with the sides cut down and are generally referred to as "A-beam" rods. These extremely light rods weigh in at only 456 grams, which is approximately 100 grams less than a standard rod of the same 6.250-inch length.

Another lightening feature of these rods is the scallops cut out of the cap side of the rod. The areas left intact are specifically located so that when two rods are bolted to the crank's rod journal they match up and proper rod side clearance is maintained.

Notice the minimal skirt area on this Mahle piston. What skirt area it has is coated to help reduce the chances of scuffing the cylinder walls. Late Model Stock rules mandate a flat-top configuration, which is fairly standard in stock car racing. Make sure your valve reliefs are no larger than necessary.

Dorton says Chevy rod bearings are wider than necessary. The extra material can potentially cause drag, so approximately 0.050 of an inch of material is cut away, at an angle, from each side in a lathe. In addition to removing surface material, the chamfer also helps ensure the bearings do not rub the extra large fillet cut into the journals of the racing crankshafts Dorton uses.

The underside of the piston is just as impressive. The pin bores have been pulled inboard to decrease the length of the wristpins. This significantly cuts weight and maintains pin rigidity. Galling between the pin and the rod is often a sign of a flexible wristpin.

The floating wristpins are held in place by wire locks, which are preferable to spiral locks because they cannot eat into the piston's lock groove if the engine experiences detonation. Dorton recommends rounding the edges on a grinding wheel to keep the locks from eating into the aluminum pistons.

The locks are simply pressed into place (carefully!) with the help of a screwdriver.

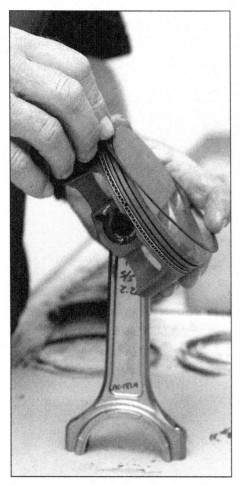

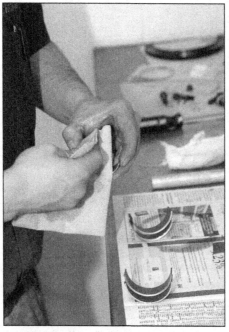

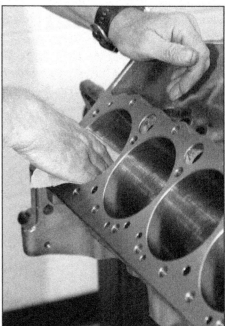

It doesn't matter how many times you've previously cleaned them, the very last thing to do before the rod bearings are placed into the rods is to wipe them down with a lint-free cloth and lacquer thinner.

During pre-fit, make sure your rod bearings are marked for the rods they are fitted to so they go back into the right places, maintaining bearing clearances. Also, notice how the extra chamfer cut into the bearings reduces surface area but does not cut into the tang (bottom).

Dorton considers ultra-low drag rings more important in a restricted-power engine than perfect, long-term oil control. The ring package for this build is 0.043-inch top and second rings and 3-mm oil rings.

Double-check to make sure the rods are properly oriented in the pistons (the chamfered side always faces the outside of the rod journal), and then give all bearings a coat of assembly lube.

Before installing any pistons, make sure the cylinder bores are absolutely clean by wiping them down with lacquer thinner on a clean, lint-free cloth. Follow that up with a light coat of motor oil or ATF fluid to prevent the bore's crosshatch from being scratched when the engine is fired up for the first time.

The piston skirts and rings are coated with light motor oil.

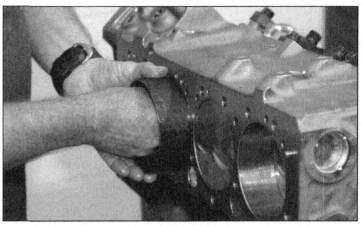

There are several different styles of ring compressors available. If you plan to build the same style engine with the same bore size again and again, a tapered ring compressor such as this is the easiest method for installing pistons in a block.

When the big end of the rod is seated against the crank's rod journal, place the cap and loosely tighten the rod bolts. Be sure to apply either extreme pressure or moly lube to the bolt threads.

You should have already determined what torque provides the proper amount of rod bolt stretch during pre-fit. Use a stretch gauge to verify this on at least the first few rod bolts. Remember, proper rod bolt stretch is usually right around 0.006 of an inch. If you go too far, loosen the bolt so that it is back in its relaxed state and measure the length again. If it is 0.001 of an inch longer than its original length in its relaxed state, that bolt is ruined.

Here's a shot of the scalloped edges on Carrillo's ultra-light connecting rods. Notice how the uncut edges still line up to maintain proper rod side clearance. Dorton says the holes created where the edges of the rod scallops meet do not create noticeable oil control problems.

While degreeing in the camshaft, Dorton can change the cam timing on this Cloyes timing set by turning an eccentric that locates the timing gear on the camshaft. It is locked in place when the three bolts holding the gear to the camshaft are tightened.

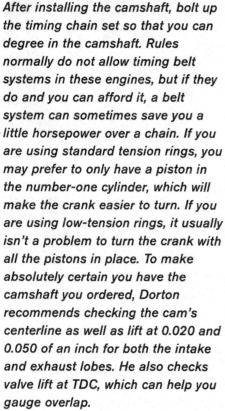

After installing the camshaft, bolt up the timing chain set so that you can degree in the camshaft. Rules normally do not allow timing belt systems in these engines, but if they do and you can afford it, a belt system can sometimes save you a little horsepower over a chain. If you are using standard tension rings, you may prefer to only have a piston in the number-one cylinder, which will make the crank easier to turn. If you are using low-tension rings, it usually isn't a problem to turn the crank with all the pistons in place. To make absolutely certain you have the camshaft you ordered, Dorton recommends checking the cam's centerline as well as lift at 0.020 and 0.050 of an inch for both the intake and exhaust lobes. He also checks valve lift at TDC, which can help you gauge overlap.

To maximize compression, the deck of the block is cut so that all pistons are between zero deck and 0.002 of an inch below at TDC.

Here's the Cloyes billet aluminum cover used with the timing set. The extra rigidity of the billet cover eliminates the need for an external cam button stop that should be used with stamped-steel covers. Also, notice that the center section of the cover is removable to make cam-timing changes easier.

When camshaft endplay is correct, the cam button location is locked down from outside the cover with a hex key. This would normally be done with the cover in place on the engine; this shot is just to illustrate how the setup works.

Here is a look at the inside of the timing cover showing how the cam button is attached to the cover. Turning the cam button in or out controls cam endplay.

Whether it is for a new engine or a rebuild, Dorton always disassembles the oil pump to check the fit of the gears. He also rubs and polishes the gears with a Scotch-Brite pad and then coats them with assembly lube before putting everything back together.

A nice coat of thick assembly lubricant on the pump gears helps prime the oil pump quickly. This ensures that the metal gears aren't grinding together while the pump tries to pull the first drops of motor oil out of the pan.

If the oil pickup separates from the pump, it means death to the engine. Because of that, the oil pickup bolts always receive a couple drops of blue Loctite to make sure they stay where they belong.

Set a straightedge across the oil pan and measure the depth to the bottom of the pan. A dial caliper works well here, but you can also use a ruler.

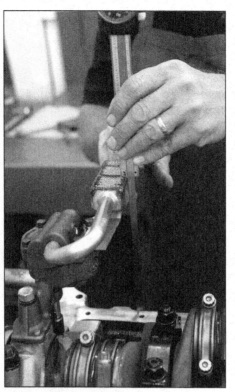

Now measure from the oil pan rail to the bottom of the oil pump pickup (it will be on top if the engine is upside down as in this photo). You should have 1/8 to 1/4 of an inch of clearance between the bottom of the pickup and the bottom of the pan. Don't forget to add in the thickness of your oil pan gasket to achieve the true clearance.

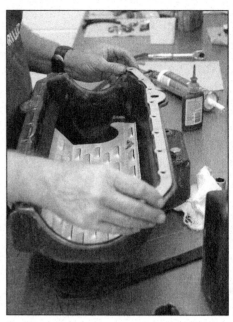

Dorton prefers to use an oil pan gasket with a steel insert. This makes it impossible to create a leak by over-tightening the oil pan bolts and distorting the gasket.

Here, the oil pan has been positioned on the block without the front gasket. Notice how the gap is greater over the center of the timing cover rail than it is on the edges. This isn't unusual, and the gap is too large to seal well using only silicone. The rubber seal that comes in most gasket kits has a uniform thickness, and if you try to bolt the pan tight enough to compress the rubber gasket on the edges enough so that the center seals up, you stand a good chance of cracking or warping the pan and creating an oil leak.

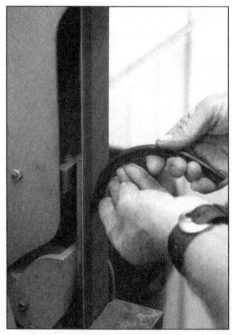

Dorton shapes the rubber gaskets on a belt sander so that the sides are thinner than the center. This requires a little bit of time and effort to be done correctly, but these gaskets are reusable so they typically will go back on after a rebuild.

Here, you can see how the modified front gasket seal properly fits between the timing cover rail and the oil pan.

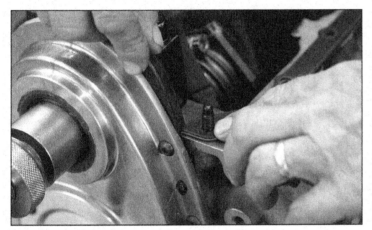

When properly trimmed, the rubber gasket and the rail gasket just butt up to one another with no overlap. A small bead of silicone provides the final seal between the two.

The "ears" on the oil pan gaskets are trimmed back so that they won't overlap the rubber front gaskets.

After a final thin bead of silicone is run over the entire gasket, the oil pan is finally ready to bolt into place.

Engine-assembly assistant Justin Bryson prepares the solid flat-tappet lifters with a liberal layer of graphite coating. Even though all flat-tappet engines are broken in on an engine dyno with lightweight break-in valvesprings, you must still take every precaution to keep the flat tappet lifters from destroying the aggressive cam lobes during the first moments after the engine is fired up.

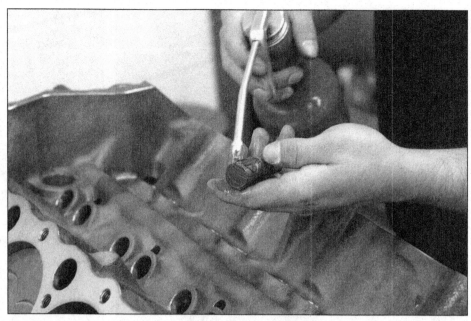

After the graphite spray dries, the face of each lifter is given another lubricant coating. This time it's a mixture of moly lube and assembly lubricant. All the cam lobes have also already been treated with the same coating.

Finally, the bodies of the lifters are thoroughly coated with motor oil before being dropped into the lifter bores.

The extra thickness of the billet timing cover requires that spacers be used on the crank pulley mandrel as well as on the water pump and power steering pump bracket.

Although MLS steel head gaskets rarely give any problems when properly torqued, Dorton takes no chances and gives both a light coating with copper head gasket spray. This further reduces the chance of a water leak.

Dorton says he has seen this plug in the side of the fuel pump body loosen and fall out. When that happens, there is nothing to stop the pin, which works as the pivot for the fuel-pump lever, from moving out of position. To prevent a fuel pump failure, he fabricates this simple metal tab, which locates on the fuel pump bolt and prevents the plug from falling out.

Another area for potential leaks is the "ears" of the head gaskets. They are given a thin coat of silicone on each side.

The assembled cylinder heads are set into place. They feature 62-cc combustion chambers, 2.020-inch intake valves, and 1.600-inch exhausts.

Shown here are the lightweight single valvesprings used for break-in on the dyno. After the engine has been broken in, the double-nested valvesprings producing 155 lbs on the seat and 400 lbs of open pressure will be installed. The race-ready lightweight steel retainers are also used with the break-in setup, as are the 7/16 screw-in rocker

The head bolts are coated with Teflon thread sealer on the threads and given a dab of extreme pressure lube underneath the head before being torqued to 70 ft-lbs. When torquing Chevy heads, begin with the center bolt and work your way around the head in a clockwise pattern spiraling outward.

The lower-right bolt holding the water pump in place threads into the water jacket. Make sure this bolt is given a dab of Teflon thread sealer or it is guaranteed to weep water.

If the intake gaskets shift during manifold installation, they can potentially block a portion of the intake tract. To prevent this, the undersides of the gaskets are given a thin coat of adhesive. After being fitted onto the intake face of the cylinder heads, Bryson gives the gaskets light taps with a flat-faced hammer to ensure that they are properly sealed to the head.

After fitting the intake gaskets, take a moment to trim away any extra gasket material—especially if any portion of the gasket intrudes into the opening for the intake ports.

After the intake gaskets are in place, test fit the manifold. There should be a gap at the front and back of the manifold that's at least 0.070 of an inch. This ensures that when the intake manifold is bolted down, it seats evenly against the intake face of the cylinder heads.

Instead of using a gasket, apply a bead of silicone to the front and rear rails of the engine to seal the underside of the intake manifold. Dorton also applies a thin coating of silicone around the port openings on the gasket to ensure a good seal.

Now you can drop the manifold in place. Most Late Model Stock rulebooks mandate a dual-plane intake manifold.

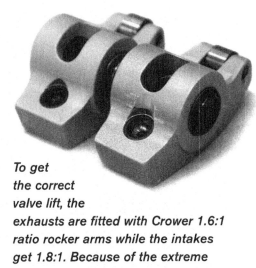

Once the correct pushrod length is determined, make sure to lubricate both ends of the pushrods before dropping them into place. Dorton also adds extreme pressure lube to the tips of the valvestems and the threads of the rocker studs.

To get the correct valve lift, the exhausts are fitted with Crower 1.6:1 ratio rocker arms while the intakes get 1.8:1. Because of the extreme ratio, the 1.8:1 intake rocker (fore-ground) has the pushrod cup moved very close to the rocker's fulcrum. With 0.650 of an inch overall intake valve lift, a little grinding is required to keep the pushrod from making contact with the rocker body. Modifi-cations like this are often necessary when building custom race engines; you just don't want to go overboard with the grinder and risk weakening the rocker arm.

Once all the rocker arms are in place, Dorton tests to make sure the flat-tappet lifters are spinning in their bores like they should. To do this he marks each of the pushrods (as you see here) and turns the engine over by hand several revolutions. The pushrods will spin with the lifters. If the marks do not move, you most likely have a cam lobe that has been improperly ground with little or no crown. This test is critical on rebuilds.

Target cold lash for this engine is 0.022 of an inch for the intake valves and 0.024 for the exhausts. The exhaust valves get more lash because they are subjected to more heat from the exhaust gasses. Dorton says that after a new build the lash will typically open up a couple thousandths, so before break-in the intake is set at 0.020 of an inch while the exhaust is tightened down at 0.022 of an inch.

If you leave the plug out of the back-side of the right lifter oil gallery, you can get a better idea of the correct distributor depth. The groove being pointed to here should be centered at the oil gallery, which you can see with the plug out of the way. Just don't forget to add the plug before firing the engine up for the first time!

Rules for this engine require stud-mounted rockers, but that doesn't mean there is nothing you can do to improve things. This stud girdle mounts across the rocker locks and does a good job of stiffening up the valvetrain. It still isn't as good as a set of shaft-mounted rockers, but it is definitely better than rocker studs alone and should help you add a few hundred RPM before valve control becomes a problem.

Most Chevy race engines use all SAE bolt sizes (in fractions of an inch), but many performance alternators use a top bracket bolt that's metric. To prevent confusion on pit road, Dorton drills the threads out of the ear on the alternator and uses a 5/16-inch nut and bolt instead.

Bryson is finally ready to bolt down the valve covers.

Dorton prefers these ribbed-style belts over more traditional V-belts for the accessory drives because they absorb less energy from the engine and are less likely to jump off the pulleys during a race.

Here's the carburetor that drives so much of this engine build. No carburetor spacer is allowed here except an adaptor plate to center the 2-barrel carb over the intake's opening. If your rulebook doesn't disallow a carb spacer, a 1-inch open or four-hole spacer certainly should help engine power.

The Spec Sheet

Engine: . . . . .NASCAR Late Model Stock
Displacement: . . . . .356 ci
Bore: 4.035
Stroke: 3.5
Compression ratio: 11.2:1

Short Block
Crankshaft: . . . . .Forged steel
Main journals: 2.45
Main bearing clearance: . . . . .0.0022 – 0.0025 in
Rod journals: 2.100
Rod bearing clearance: . . . . .0.0018 – 0.0022 in
Connecting Rods: . . . . .Forged A-beam
Rod length: 6.250
Pin size: 927
Rod bolt size: 3/8
Pistons: . . . . .Forged aluminum flat-top
Rings: . . . . .0.043 in, 0.043 in & 3.0 mm
Deck Height: 8.995
Piston compression distance: 1.00
Piston height: . . . . .0.002 in hole
Oiling: . . . . .Wet sump

Cylinder Head
Head: . . . . .Cast iron Bow Tie
Intake valve: 2.020
Exhaust valve: 1.600
Combustion Chamber: .62 cc
Head bolts: 7/16

Valvetrain
Camshaft: . . . . .Cast
Lifters: . . . . .Solid flat tappet, 0.843 diameter
Pushrods: . . . . .3/8 diameter, 0.080 wall
Rockers: . . . . .1.8:1 intake
. . . . .1.6:1 exhaust
Valve lift: . . . . .0.650 intake, 0.578 exhaust
Lobe lift: 0.361
Duration: . . . . .246 intake, 254 exhaust @ 0.050
Valve Lash: . . . . .0.022 intake, 0.024 exhaust cold

Ignition
Ignition: . . . . .Distributor with coil and external box
Firing order: . . . . .Standard
Plug gap: 0.030

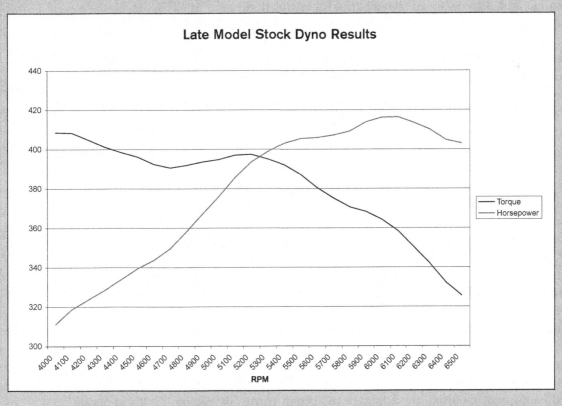

DIRT LATE MODEL ENGINE BUILD

The no-holds-barred Dirt Late Model engine is one of the most viciously powerful in all of stock car racing. With 800-plus HP, it boasts nearly as much peak power as a NASCAR Nextel Cup powerplant, but the DLM engine works over a much wider RPM range and, thanks to an aluminum block, also weighs significantly less.

The DLM engine easily produces the most power and torque of our three engine builds. This is due to having the most cubic inches, a healthy 14.5:1 compression ratio, and a host of custom-made speed parts. The drawback is that this motor is also by far the most expensive, averaging between $30,000 and $40,000, depending on the builder and parts used. It also takes the most time to build, partly because it requires much custom fabrication.

To be frank, a full-bore DLM engine is probably outside the range of most non-professional engine builders. This is not because of the skills that must be mastered, but because of the many different pieces of specialized equipment required to complete the job. Still, it is possible to do the assembly yourself if you can farm out some of the machine work. And even if you never build your own DLM engine, there are a lot of tips here that you can take advantage of in any engine you build.

Clements Racing Engines in Spartanburg, South Carolina, is the builder of our full-bore DLM mill. Clements specializes in dirt racing, especially the Late Models, and even has its own CNC machining centers in-house, which it uses to turn raw cylinder head castings into pieces of automotive jewelry. Clements has worked with many of the top DLM racers in the country and produces approximately 250 engines a year.

The engine for this build is a Chevrolet SB2. Originally developed in 1996 for NASCAR Nextel Cup (then called Winston Cup) competition, the SB2 has since been adopted by other forms of racing

Clements Racing Engines' all-aluminum Dirt Late Model engine takes advantage of a very thin rulebook to make in excess of 840 hp and 650 ft-lbs of torque.

because it is a more efficient design than the classic small block. The SB2 (which means Small Block Second Generation) has actually been updated since its inception and is now officially called the SB2.2, but most racers still refer to it simply as the SB2.

The SB2 (both versions) is based on the original small block, but it has a few critical differences. First, the valve pattern is different. Instead of a valve pattern with the exhausts on the outside edges (E, I, I, E, E, I, I, E) like a standard Chevy small-block, the SB2 moves the intake valves to the outside (I, E, I, E, E, I, E, I). This is called a "Mirror Pattern" and the intake ports are angled toward the center of the engine to provide a straighter path for the air/fuel charge from the carburetor to the combustion chambers.

The valve angles have also decreased significantly from our 23-degree Street Stock. In this form, the intake valves are at 11 degrees with a 4-degree sideways cant to reduce valve shrouding. The exhaust valves, meanwhile, are angled at eight degrees from vertical.

In addition, the lifter bores are offset for the intake versus the exhaust lifters. This change in angles cleans up the rocker arm geometry and eliminates the need for offset rockers, which are expensive and can cause wear problems. Coolant flow throughout the motor, especially to the cylinder heads, is also improved. Finally, the SB2 is a dry-sump-only engine since there is no oil filter boss on the block casting.

The biggest drawback to the SB2 engine for racing is the cost. The engine is well supported by the aftermarket, but since it is expressly designed for ultra-high performance

racing, there is virtually nothing on the economical end of the spectrum for it. Glenn Clements says that it costs Clements Racing Engines approximately $6,000 more to build an SB2 than it does a similarly sized Chevrolet small-block. But a well-built SB2 will always be capable of producing more power than a first-generation small-block, so for most teams the extra cost simply comes down to a matter of whether it can be worked into the budget.

The Block

Another unique factor of this build is that this is the first time we are using a block not produced by General Motors. The DLM rulebook is surprisingly open, so Clements sources an aluminum SB2 block by Dart. The Dart block arrives with several features that can make an engine builder's life a little easier. For example, the freeze plug holes arrive with threads cut to accept screw-in freeze plugs. These plugs use O-rings to virtually eliminate leaks. The cam bore is also raised to allow for stroker applications, which Clements regularly takes advantage of.

This particular engine will be given a 4.00-inch stroke, and along with a final bore diameter of 4.145 inches will have a displacement of 431 cubic inches. Even though the block is designed to accommodate extra crankshaft throw, that kind of long stroke still requires a little extra work cutting clearance for the counterweights.

An aluminum engine block requires cast iron cylinder sleeves no matter if you are racing an SB2 or a standard small-block. Glenn Clements and engine builder Chuck Pridgeon say they have noticed that some-

times the sleeves won't be fully seated from the foundry, and this is true for any brand of aluminum engine block. When this is the case, the sleeve will eventually settle, which can lead to cylinder sealing problems. To counteract this potential problem, Clements says you should find some way to ensure that every sleeve is completely seated before decking the block.

Clements Automotive uses a homemade tool that seats against the main bearing housing bore at one end and the corresponding cylinder sleeve, on the deck, on the other. The two sides are connected by a large piece of threaded rod, which can be used to compress the tool and ensure the sleeve is completely seated. After all the sleeves have been treated to this process, the cylinders are honed before the block is decked.

Rotating Assembly

The rotating assembly swings on a custom 4.00-inch stroke crank created for Clements Automotive by Crower Cams and Equipment. The forged crank uses pendulum-cut counterweights to help achieve proper balance with minimum overall weight.

Although the typical DLM rulebook might allow ultra-small journal sizes like you will find in a Nextel Cup engine, you might be surprised to see the larger, relatively standard size main and rod journals on this crank. The mains measure 3.500 inches while the rod journals are Chevrolet standard at 2.100 inches. The extra beef is necessary because of both the large quantities of torque this engine puts out and because most DLM teams simply cannot afford to rebuild their engines after every race like a Cup team. This engine, in fact, is expected to run between 1,000 and 1,200 laps before a rebuild is required. Main bearing clearance is maintained between 0.0018 and 0.0021 of an inch.

The rods are 6.00 inches from center to center and produced by Dyer's Top Rods. A 6-inch rod is about all you can pack into the block with a 9.00-inch deck height, when combined with a 4-inch stroke. Even at that length, the piston pin intrudes into the oil ring land and requires a few extra precautions.

Rod bearing clearance is held between 0.0024 and 0.0026 of an inch, but Pridgeon looks for that clearance in a very specific location. The big end of the rod flexes and deforms slightly into an oval shape every time the crank pulls the rod and piston down into the bore on the induction stroke. Because of this, Pridgeon measures the rod journal housing bore vertically (parallel to the beam of the rod) and 45 degrees to either side. If the vertical clearance is correct, the variance at the 45-degree measurements is allowed to be larger by as much as 0.0005 of an inch, but no smaller then the vertical measurement. For example, if the crank's rod journal measures exactly 2.100, then the housing bore of the rod with the bearing in place should measure no less than 2.1024. The bore diameter 45 degrees from vertical may be as much as 2.1029 inches, but if it is any smaller than the target size of 2.1024, the rod must be re-honed.

The pistons receive the greatest amount of work. In order to reach the 14.5:1 compression ratio, the pistons have a small dome. They are quite beefy with a full skirt, which Pridgeon says is necessary in order to live in an 800-hp environment for 1,200 laps. The 1.00-inch compression distance is so short that the pin bore intrudes into the oil-ring land, and the oil ring requires its own support rail. Finally, to maximize ring seal in the bores, which is an area of abuse for most dirt motors, each piston has eight gas ports cut into the top ring land. The ports are cut so that half of the 0.060-inch drill bit cuts into the aluminum that forms the top of the ring land while the other half is in the gap of the land. These ports allow combustion pressure to get behind the rings and press them outward, improving ring seal against the cylinder walls. Once all of that is done, every surface of the piston must be massaged with a Scotch-Brite pad to eliminate any sharp edges that may cause detonation.

Valvetrain

Clements uses a custom ground cam supplied by Comp Cams with a 55-mm core for ultimate rigidity. The cam spins in the bore on roller bearings for extra protection, and a gear set from Shaver-Wesmar controls the timing. This is necessary because the aluminum block undergoes so much thermal expansion that a traditional timing chain can cause valve control problems. The Shaver-Wesmar gear set maintains good control even with the extreme expansion inherent in the aluminum block. It is also quite durable when set up correctly.

One of the strengths of the SB2.2 engine is the revised valve angles, but this also creates a few unique requirements. For example, the lifter bores are offset, which requires special matching lifter sets. The SB2 lifters are solid rollers supplied by Crower and are oversized to 0.937-inch diameter to allow all the largest rollers possible. The lifters activate the 1.75:1 shaft-mount rockers through 7/16 inch, 0.165-wall pushrods, which are two different lengths because of the lifter-bore offset.

Ignition

Another unique facet of this motor is its crank-trigger controlled ignition. Clements uses the crank trigger because it is more precise than using the distributor to control spark timing. This is because there are lots of opportunities for tolerances to stack or flex to be introduced between the crankshaft, timing assembly, camshaft, distributor gear, and finally the distributor. These variances are more than enough to significantly affect when the spark ignites the air/fuel mixture.

A crank trigger assembly eliminates nearly all of those mechanical connections. It is connected directly to the snout of the crank and uses a magnetic pickup to signal the ignition exactly when to fire each spark plug. Proof that this system can be beneficial shows up not only on the dyno, but also when setting the engine timing. In many cases you can see that the timing is much more stable when shining a timing light on the advance scale scribed on the side of the balancer.

Although Clements sometimes experiments with different firing orders for their Chevrolet engines, this SB2 utilizes a standard 1, 8, 4, 3, 6, 5, 7, 2 firing order. The spark plugs are gapped to 0.035 of an inch.

As you can see, the roller cam bearings are installed just after the machine work is completed. In addition to reducing rotational friction, roller bearings for the camshaft provide a little additional protection from the intense spring pressures trying to push the cam into the cam bores.

One of the easiest ways to identify an SB2.2 block is the offset lifter bores. These clean up the valvetrain angles and eliminate the need for offset rocker arms.

The use of studs to clamp the cylinder heads and main caps is always preferable over bolts in an aluminum block. This is because, unlike bolts, the studs are threaded into place with no stress. The clamping load is provided when the nuts are torqued into place. The outside holes on the second, third, and fourth caps are splayed, however, and require bolts.

Whenever you use an aluminum block, there is a chance that the cast iron cylinder sleeves may settle after the engine goes through a few heat cycles. If this happens, the engine will suffer coolant leaks, a loss of combustion pressure, and a blown head gasket probably isn't far behind.

To ensure that the iron cylinder sleeves are fully seated, Clements uses this homemade tool that seats against the saddle of the main bore and squeezes the cylinder sleeve into the block. The block is not decked until all boring and honing procedures are finished.

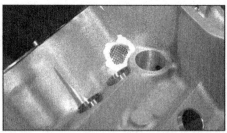

Screw-in freeze plugs virtually eliminate the possibility that a leaky plug will spill coolant on the track in front of your rear tires at the worst possible time.

Since this block is intended for high-end competition use only, there are no oil drain-back holes cast in the lifter valley above the camshaft. Oil from the cylinder heads can drain back to the pan through holes at the front and rear of the lifter valley. This is done to eliminate power-robbing windage caused by oil coming into contact with the crank.

The Crower crank uses pendulum-cut counterweights to minimize total weight, but it still is rather hefty. Although they have the option to go smaller, Clements uses 3.500-inch main journals and Chevy-standard 2.100-inch rod journals. This is necessary to prevent breakage, as these motors will see a lot of laps before they come back for a rebuild.

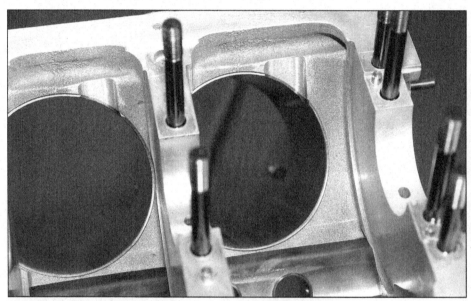

The crank's four-inch stroke also means extra clearance must be cut inside the block. The obsructions here are the counterweights, not the connecting rods

One engine-building trick Pridgeon uses is to vary the torque on the main caps to get exactly the main bearing clearance he is looking for. The torque on the main studs and bolts can safely vary as much as 10 lbs, so actual torque on the main studs can be between 65 and 75 ft-lbs without a problem. After torquing all the mains to 70 ft-lbs with the bearings installed, he measures for clearance.

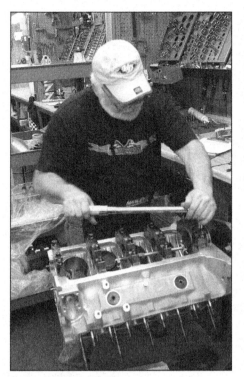

The billet steel camshaft is slid into place. Glenn Clements says that one of the most difficult aspects of building a quality DLM engine is camshaft selection, because racers demand big power over a wide RPM range. Clements Racing Engines spends more R&D time on the camshaft than just about anything else, and the specifics are a closely guarded secret.

If the bearing clearance is a couple of thousandths too small, Pridgeon says he will decrease the torque as much as five ft-lbs and re-measure. If the clearance is too loose, he can increase the torque on the nuts on the main studs as much as five ft-lbs.

Once he's found what works best, Pridgeon writes the torque value for each stud beside the cap on the oil pan rail. Now he knows exactly what values he needs during final assembly.

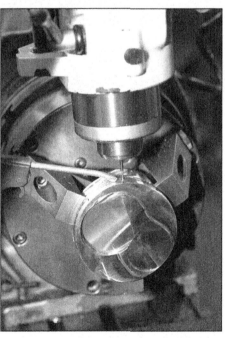

Here's the finished product. The ports allow combustion gasses to get behind the top ring and push it out against the cylinder wall to provide improved sealing. This is effective even when the ring is worn.

Each piston has eight gas ports cut in the top of the top ring land to aid ring seal. Before cutting, the location for each port is marked on the piston. This is done to ensure no gas port is near the intake valve pocket closest to the edge of the piston.

The ports are cut on a mill under a constant stream of air to keep heat from warping the ring land.

Each 0.927-inch diameter wristpin receives a diamond-hard Casidiam coating to prevent galling against either the rod bushing or the piston's pin bore. This is necessary because in a dry-sump engine very little oil reaches the wristpin.

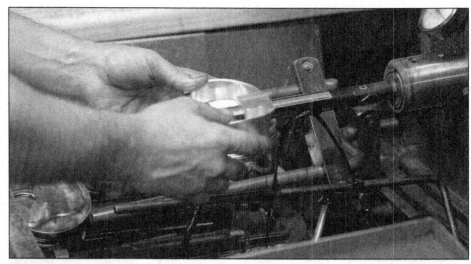

All of the piston pin bores receive a mild honing to improve oil retention between the pin and the piston's pin bore.

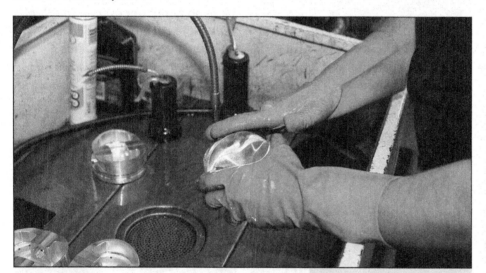

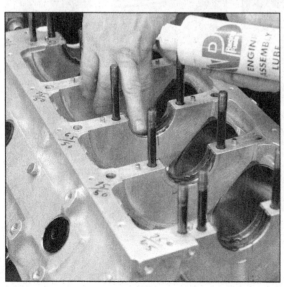

Once the alterations are complete, every surface of the piston is rubbed with a Scotch-Brite pad. This ensures there are no rough spots left behind that can cause detonation.

The main bearing surfaces are coated with assembly lube in preparation for the crank.

The connecting rods are 6-inch H-beam rods from Dyer's Top Rods. Pridgeon prefers 0.0024 to 0.0026 of an inch rod clearance.

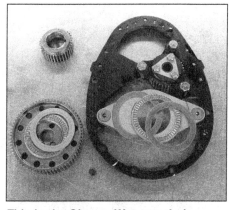

This is the Shaver-Wesmar timing gear setup Clements uses for all of its aluminum-block race motors.

Because this is a dry-sump engine, a special rear oil seal is used, which is installed directly on the crank. This seal uses two lips to keep oil inside the engine as well as prevent outside air from intruding due to oil pump vacuum.

After dropping the crank into place, Pridgeon torques the mains to the specs determined earlier. Crank endplay is checked and should be between 0.003 and 0.006 of an inch.

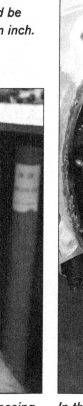

Pridgeon uses sealant on both sides of a timing cover gasket before pressing the gear drive into place. This is done to eliminate leaks caused by the different expansion rates of the aluminum block and the steel frame ring of the gear drive.

In these photos the crank gear is already pressed into position. The frame holds the idler gear.

The metal plate serves as a thrust plate for the camshaft, and bolts across the front of the gear drive frame.

Once everything is in place, Pridgeon checks camshaft endplay. When the engine is cold there should be no free play from end to end, but it should not be so tight that the cam feels bound up.

The cam timing gear slides into place and bolts directly to the camshaft with its teeth contacting the idler gear. A roller thrust bearing is coated with high-pressure lube before being pressed into place on the face of the cam gear. The bronze bushing in the cam gear allows for timing adjustments.

Adding or removing shims between the camshaft and the cam gear can adjust clearance.

After connecting the crankshaft to the cam with the timing set, Pridgeon checks the cam timing. Notice the homemade tool that allows him to check both the intake and exhaust lobes at the same time. One of the features of this block is a raised cam tunnel that allows for longer stroke packages. Unfortunately, this also means any timing marks on the timing set are invalid.

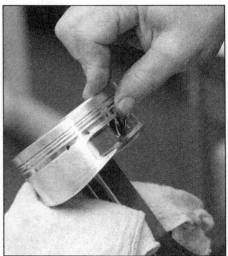

The pistons are installed on the connecting rods, and wire locks are used to hold the floating wristpins in position.

Pridgeon has come up with an interesting tool to help install the locks. It is simply an old wristpin of the same size with a second pin welded in place as a T-handle.

Once the wire lock is placed in the edge of the pin bore, the end of the tool is used to push the wire lock in until it locks in its groove.

Coated bearings are used on both the rods and main caps. Most engine builders agree that they don't help a race engine produce extra power. However, they do provide an extra measure of security against a spun bearing if the oil pressure unexpectedly dips for a second or two.

The piston rings are 1.2-mm thick for the top and second rings and 3-mm for the oil rings. The top two are both gapped at 0.016 of an inch while the oil rings are gapped to at least 0.010. Pridgeon says that they have to be tight when cold because the expansion rate of the aluminum block is so great. In practice, he says he wants the oil-ring gap about as tight as he can get it. As long as the ends of the rings aren't butting when trial fit in the cylinder bore, he's happy.

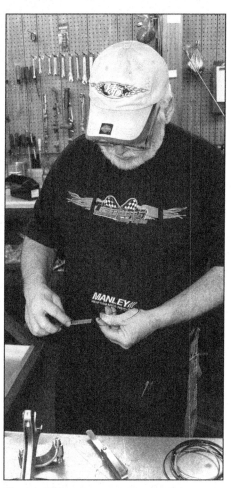

Once all the rings are properly gapped, the edges are touched up with a file to make sure there are no burrs that can affect fit.

Notice the extremely short compression distance on this piston, and how the pin bore extends into the oil-ring land. Because of this, a support ring (shown here) is installed before the actual oil rings and the expander.

Pridgeon installs the rings on the pistons, making sure the end gaps between the rings are at least 90 degrees apart.

Take a couple of precautions to protect the pistons and cylinder bores before installation. First, wipe down the cylinder bores with a lint-free towel dampened with lacquer thinner to cut any greases in the bore.

Coat the rod bearings liberally with assembly lube. Too much here makes a mess, but too little can allow the babbitt to be torn off of the bearing face.

Lubricate the rings and piston skirts to protect them from galling in the bore when the engine is first fired up. Pridgeon chooses to use automatic transmission fluid here instead of motor oil, saying that it leaves less residue in the cylinder bore.

Use a ring compressor to tap the pistons into place, making sure the chamfered side of the rod faces the outside edge of the rod journal.

Pridgeon uses high-pressure lube on the rod bolts because he says it is more consistent than moly lube.

Remember, the torque number to properly fasten the rod bolts will vary depending on whether you use high-pressure lube, moly lube, or even regular motor oil. More important is getting the proper stretch, usually 0.006 of an inch.

Connecting rod side clearance is checked with a feeler gauge. Pridgeon looks for between 0.015 and 0.020 of an inch. This may sound relatively loose, but it doesn't affect the oil's level of protection for the rod bearings. Pridgeon says he has noticed that the oil heats up more when the rod side clearance is tighter.

Once assembled, the height of each piston is checked. The target for each is to be between zero deck and 0.005 in the hole.

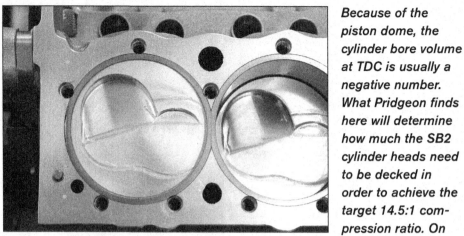

Because of the piston dome, the cylinder bore volume at TDC is usually a negative number. What Pridgeon finds here will determine how much the SB2 cylinder heads need to be decked in order to achieve the target 14.5:1 compression ratio. On an SB2 head, normally cutting 0.0055 of an inch off the deck will remove 1cc from the combustion chambers.

Because each piston has been worked so much from its box-stock form, the cylinder volume is checked with the piston at TDC.

Once the rotating assembly is complete, the bottom end is buttoned up with a dry-sump oil pan from Dan Olson Racing Products.

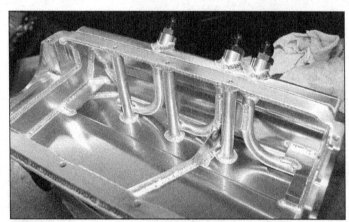

A good dry-sump pan is a big departure from most top-end wet-sump oil pans. Here, the best design is relatively open with no kickouts and not even a windage tray. The idea is to allow the oil to drop to the bottom of the pan as quickly as possible, so that the oil pump can draw it out through one of the three pickups and get it out of the way.

Notice that the pan does have the left-side wall moved out past the end of the pan rail to reduce the opportunity for oil to bounce off the wall of the pan and make contact with the spinning crankshaft. This means the bolts holding the pan on must be inserted through holes in the bottom of the pan and plugs used to seal the holes.

Before assembly onto the block, cylinder head specialist Lance Evatt taps the oil drain-back holes in the head to accept a 1/8-inch restrictor. These restrictors cause the valve covers to flood with oil at racing RPM levels, which helps keep the valvesprings cool.

Almost all high-end engines need multi-layer steel head gaskets for the improved seal they provide. Pridgeon takes it a step further by applying a thin layer of high-temp silicone around all the cooling holes to ensure the gasket stays sealed.

After decking the heads to achieve the correct combustion chamber volume for the target compression ratio, they are ready to be put in place.

Notice the ultra-light titanium retainers used with the valvesprings. They are expensive but generally considered a mandatory upgrade on a high-end engine such as this. The weight savings over steel will allow the engine a couple extra hundred RPM before the springs lose valve control.

Because of the SB2's offset lifter bores, a set of roller lifters requires two different styles of tie bars. These Crower 0.937-inch lifter sets are marked for which cylinders each works with.

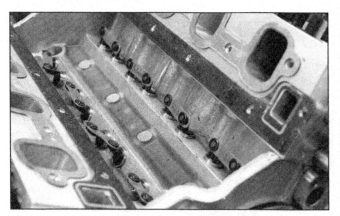

As long as the tie bars are facing the center of the lifter valley, it's impossible to put them in the wrong bores. Make sure to fully soak the lifters in motor oil before installing them in the block.

Before the T&D rockers can be installed, the rocker stand must be bolted down and the pushrods installed.

For this engine, Clements is using 8.900-inch pushrods for the intakes and 9.00-inch pushrods for the exhausts. The pushrods have a large 7/16 diameter with a 0.165-inch wall to minimize flex.

Before assembly, each of the adjuster caps is given a small dab of high-pressure lube.

The rocker shafts have a flat side and a rounded side. The rounded side should fit perfectly into the stands.

The lash is set at zero cold, so once the rocker is bolted to the stand, Pridgeon simply tightens the lash cap while spinning the pushrod until he feels pressure.

The steel T&D rockers feature a priority oiling system that takes oil feed from the pushrod, through the adjuster nut, and on to the fulcrum and the roller tip.

Because the Dart block has a raised cam tunnel, metal shims have to be welded in place to achieve proper distributor height.

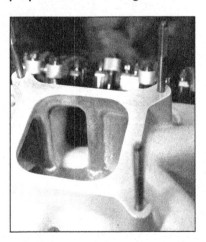

The intake manifold has already been port matched to the intake ports in the cylinder heads, so it's just a matter of getting everything lined up before bolting it down tight. Once in place the distributor can be installed.

Although the crank trigger determines spark timing, the distributor is still needed to route the spark to the proper plug. It is also used as a backup in case there is a failure of the crank trigger during a race. It is wired so the driver only needs to throw a switch to change over.

The cast valley cover bolts into place next.

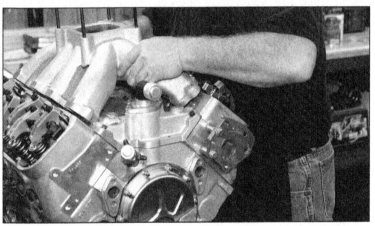

The union between the intake manifold and the cylinder heads is not under extreme pressure, so Pridgeon applies a light coat of moly lube to the intake manifold face. This allows the intake to be removed without destroying the gasket, which can be used again.

Before installing the crank trigger pickup, the engine is adjusted so that the number-one piston is 30 degrees BTDC (the position when the plug should fire). The pickup is positioned next to the closest magnet on the blue flywheel (behind the crank pulley) and, using a feeler gauge, positioned so that it is only 0.050 of an inch away.

The valve covers feature integrated valvespring oilers, which spray a pressurized mist of oil on each spring to help keep them cool.

A restrictor with a 0.045-inch hole that screws into the inlet controls oil pressure inside the rail. If you look closely, you can see that the orifice is actually a carburetor air bleed.

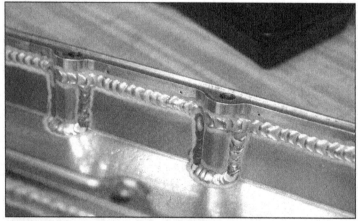

The oil actually travels inside the rail on the bottom of the valve cover, and tiny holes drilled into the rail aim the oil at each of the valvesprings.

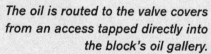

The oil is routed to the valve covers from an access tapped directly into the block's oil gallery.

The Spec Sheet

Engine: . . . . .Unlimited Dirt Late Model
Displacement: . . . . .431 ci
Bore: 4.145
Stroke: 4.00
Compression ratio: 14.5:1

Short Block
Crankshaft: . . . . .Forged steel
Main journals: 3.500
Main bearing clearance: 0.0018-0.0021
Rod journals: 2.100
Rod bearing clearance: 0.0021-0.0026
Connecting Rods: . . . . .Forged H-beam
Rod length: 6.00
Pin size: 0.927
Rod bolt size: 7/16
Pistons: . . . . .Forged aluminum with dome
Rings: . . . . .1.2 mm, 1.2 mm, 3.0 mm
Deck Height: 9.00
Piston compression distance: 1.00
Piston height: . . . . .0 deck to 0.004 in hole
Oiling: . . . . .Dry sump with external pump

Cylinder Head
Head: . . . . .SB2.2 aluminum
Intake valve: 2.180
Exhaust valve: 1.600
Combustion Chamber: . . . . .47.5 cc
Head bolts: . . . . .3/8 outside, 7/16 center

Valvetrain
Camshaft: . . . . .Billet steel
Lifters: . . . . .Solid roller, 0.937 diameter
Pushrods: . . . . .7/16 diameter, 0.165 wall
Rockers: . . . . .1.75:1 steel shaft mount
Valve lift: 0.760
Lobe lift: 0.434
Duration: . . . . .265 @ 0.050
Valve Lash: . . . . .0 cold

Ignition
Ignition: . . . . .Crank trigger
Firing order: . . . . .Standard
Plug gap: 0.035

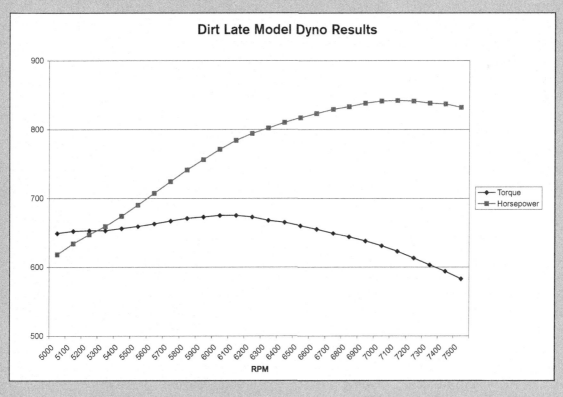

BREAK-IN, REGULAR MAINTENANCE, AND TEARDOWN

You've put a lot of money and effort into building your engine, and you have finally reached the payoff: it's time to race!

Of course, you also want to make sure your investment makes maximum power for as long as possible and runs dependably race after race. This is where a good maintenance program comes in. A few simple checks done regularly can help you spot any developing problems before they become expensive ones. It can also help you avoid engine failures that are guaranteed to ruin an otherwise good night of racing.

Your maintenance plan should include proper engine break-in and an engine refresh and rebuild schedule. Break-in is critical because all those new components have to be allowed to gently mesh together before you start applying the big power, and should be done for every new engine. On the other side of the spectrum, how often you rebuild your race engine depends on the type of parts used, the engine's power level, and the length of races you run. Ultra-light parts obviously

aren't as durable as more solidly built components, so if you have opted for the lightweight go-fast stuff you should be prepared to rebuild more often. Most 400 to 500 hp stock car race engines, when well-built, can last an entire season between rebuilds. High-horsepower engines, and schedules that have you regularly running 200-plus lap features, may mean tearing into the engine twice a year or more.

The best thing you can do to ensure engine longevity is to start keeping a log of every lap your race-car makes on the track, whether in race conditions, testing, or practice. Use this information to set up a timetable in terms of laps run between rebuilds. It is impossible to tell you here how many laps you can run, but you can get a good feel for what's best for you by talking to other racers in your class and even local engine builders. This, of course, is in addition to paying attention to how your engine sounds and performs on the racetrack, as well as keeping a close eye on your gauges. Odd sounds, a drop in oil pressure,

or a loss of power may all necessitate an investigatory engine rebuild.

Break-In

Many racing classes still require flat-tappet camshaft and lifter combinations. This is mainly because these components are still cheaper than roller cam combinations, and it

Flat-tappet lifters are still common in stock car racing. They pose challenges to the engine builder because of the friction created by the tappet face sliding up the cam lobe.

Here is the result from an engine that wasn't properly broken in. The shiny cam lobe has been "wiped," meaning the crown of the lobe that causes the flat-tappet lifter to spin in its bore has been ground off. This cam is now trash.

is also an easy way to limit power. But as race engine builders and parts manufacturers have continued to push the performance limits of these components, the stresses placed on the camshaft lobe and lifter tappet have increased greatly.

There are several factors that make it more difficult than ever to get an engine with a flat-tappet camshaft to survive the first critical hour of operation. As engine performance has increased over time, camshaft designers have been forced to design lobe ramps that open and close the valves incredibly quickly. The diameter of a flat-tappet lifter limits the opening ramp speed of the camshaft lobe. Lobes have gotten more radical, but lifter diameters have been constrained by the rules and haven't been allowed to grow to handle it. To get the maximum available power, camshaft designers are always working around that line where the edge of the lifter will dig into the side of the lobe.

A second factor is the stronger valvesprings that are being used to keep the valvetrain under control at very high RPM levels. The stronger spring increases the pressure between the tappet and the lobe, and any loss

of lubricant film between the two surfaces can be damaging.

To make matters worse, most modern over-the-counter oils aren't formulated with an emphasis on sliding friction inhibitors because OEM engines don't use flat-tappet camshafts anymore. Because of this, if you just crank up your newly built flat-tappet race engine and go, you are virtually guaranteed to destroy the camshaft.

Better Oil

We've already stated that most motor oils aren't formulated to handle the sliding friction produced when a tappet lifter slides up and over a camshaft lobe. Though an over-simplification, many engine builders refer to the component missing from modern oils that help sliding friction as "zinc," after the primary component. One of the reasons zinc has largely been removed is because it clogs oxygen sensors.

The solution is to look for oils that are formulated specifically for racing. These normally contain additional zinc or phosphorus, which are excellent for protecting against high-pressure sliding friction. Another option is to use an oil additive. Comp Cams sells an additive designed to protect the camshaft and lifters during break-in, but it can also provide additional protection to racing engines with no harm over long-term use.

The Break-In Process

Properly breaking in a flat-tappet engine normally requires running it for 45 minutes to one hour at around 2,000 rpm without loading or otherwise putting any strain on the engine. If the engine is on a dyno, this means no pulls. If the engine is in

your racecar, keep the car in neutral or have the rear end sitting on jack stands so the wheels can spin freely. The engine shouldn't be allowed to idle for any length of time. At idle speeds, the oil pump cannot provide enough oil pressure through the

Go Diesel

Ever thought about using diesel oil in your high-tech race engine? No, I didn't think so.

The engineers at Comp Cams recently performed exhaustive research on engine oils to determine how well they protect flat-tappet camshafts. As you might expect, many failed the test, but some of those that passed might surprise you.

According to Comp, "Because of the more severe loads in diesel applications, many of the better diesel-use motor oils have high pressure friction inhibitors as good or better than any of the previous automotive oils. The current API ratings to look for are CI-4 Plus, CI-4, and CF-4. Oils that meet these standards should be recommended at least through the flat-tappet break-in period along with Comp Cams' Camshaft Break-In Lube oil additive."

As this book went to press, some of the diesel oils that meet this criterion include Castrol Tection Extra SAE 15W-40, Chevron Delo 400 Multigrade SAE 15W-40, Mobil Delvac 1300 Super 15W-40, and Shell Rotella T Multigrade SAE 15W-40.

Priming an internal oil pump isn't difficult. You can either purchase a tool that engages and spins the oil pump driveshaft with the help of a power drill (shown here), or you can make your own with on old distributor. Remove everything from the distributor except for the housing and the distributor shaft. Install it as you normally would a distributor and then spin the shaft with a drill.

Prime the engine until you see oil exiting the priority oiling feed holes in the rocker arms. This ensures that you have oil pressure in all the galleries inside the block as well as inside the pushrods. Now the engine will be able to adequately oil all critical areas as soon as it fires up.

engine. Instead, keep the engine at around 2,000 rpm, occasionally varying the RPM between 1,500 and 2,500.

Before firing the engine for the first time, it is also necessary to make a few modifications. First, since the RPM will be limited and the engine won't be under load, there is no reason to use the full spring pressure. When breaking in an engine, use a set of "break-in springs," which are available from most spring manufacturers, or, if you are using a double-nested spring, use just the outer spring.

During break-in, you should aim for spring pressures between 100 to 120 lbs on the seat (but never less than 80) and approximately 280 lbs over the nose (but never more than 300). Running your normal spring pressures during break-in is a sure way to wipe a lobe. The pressure of the springs pressing the lifter into the cam lobe before proper break-in simply grinds off the nose of the lobe.

Also, before cranking the engine for the first time, don't forget to spin the oil pump to pressurize the oiling system. You can do this with a drill, spinning a special tool designed to engage the oil pump driveshaft. Don't make the mistake of spinning the pump only until you see the needle on the oil pressure gauge move. The oil pressure sending unit is normally somewhere along the main oil gallery. Just because you have oil pressure there doesn't mean you have oil pressure inside the lifter galleries, in the lifters, up the pushrods, or in the rocker arms.

Instead, pull the valve covers and spin the oil pump until you see oil coming out of the oiling hole of every rocker arm. You may have to slowly spin the engine over with a wrench to get oil through all the lifters. If this is too much trouble, continue spinning the oil pump for five minutes after you see movement on the oil pressure gauge.

When you do finally crank the engine, make sure that you are absolutely ready. Ideally, you want it to fire up as soon as you hit the starter. The worst thing you can do is to spin the motor over for a minute or two without it firing. When the engine does fire, be ready to go straight into your break-in ritual. All adjustments should already have been made.

After Break-In Checks

During the break-in run, you should always keep an attentive eye on the engine. Listen for changes in how it's running. You can also occasionally check to make sure all the headers are hot, which will let you know you don't have a dead cylinder.

In stock classes you may be required to run ball-fulcrum rockers such as these. If the engine's oil galleries aren't primed all the way to the rockers, they can be starved of oil and the assembly lube burned off before engine oil is supplied through the pushrods. The result is a burnt fulcrum as you can see here.

After the 45 minutes of break-in is complete, shut the engine down and allow it to cool. Begin your post break-in checkup by looking at the filters to make sure you don't have excess metal particles in the filter media. There is more information on how to do this in the Regular Maintenance section of this chapter.

Next, re-lash the valves and note how much they have changed. There should be some settling as the assembly lube is washed into the pan and the valvetrain components mate together, which causes the lash to open up. If, however, the lash moves by more than 0.005 of an inch, there is cause for concern.

If you have this situation, perform a quick pushrod check. On the valve with too much lash, mark a vertical line near the top of the pushrod and spin the motor several times. Watch the line. If the pushrod spins, then that means the

cam lobe and lifter are probably still okay. If it doesn't, that's a good sign that the crown on the nose of the cam lobe has been ground off, or "wiped." If this is the case, the cam has been ruined and will need to be replaced.

Once everything checks out okay, it is time to bring your engine to race-ready status. Install the full-pressure spring set you plan to race with. Next, drain the engine oil and replace it with racing oil and, finally, install a fresh oil filter. It's time to go racing!

Regular Maintenance

Between rebuilds there are a few very important steps you can take to keep tabs on the health of your engine. The idea here is to catch problems in the early stages, before they cause a component failure. The good news is that everything listed here can be done with the engine in the racecar.

Check the Valve Lash

I already explained the procedure for checking valve lash in the chapter on cylinder head preparation, so it won't be covered again here. If you are running solid lifters, it is important to check your valve lash after every race, or at least after every other race. Even if your adjusters are locked down tight, your valve lash will change with time.

With normal engine use, you can expect valve lash to slowly decrease. In other words, the gap between the rocker arm and the valvestem tip when the lifter for that rocker is on the base circle of the camshaft will get smaller. This is because of wear between the valve and the valve seat, which allows the valve to sit higher in the head. This should be considered a normal wear pattern and isn't cause for concern unless you have one valve that moves by more than a couple thousandths after a race.

When checking lash, remember that expansion from heat will cause the valve lash on a warm engine to be different from one that's at room temperature. To get the most accurate measurements, it is a good idea to run the engine long enough to allow it to fully warm up. Pull one valve cover and check just the lash for one cylinder head. After that, warm the engine up again and repeat the process on the other side.

If you notice the lash has opened up or grown larger than the last time you checked, the problem is likely a wiped lobe on the camshaft or a failed lifter. If you are running roller lifters, the failure is usually a broken roller axle or the bearings that allow the roller to spin smoothly have been crushed.

If, however, you notice the lash for one or more valves opening up, you definitely should investigate further. The most common reason for a gain in valve lash is failure of either the cam lobe or the lifter. If you are running flat-tappet lifters, especially with an aggressive racing cam, lobe wear is a constant enemy.

Properly breaking in the camshaft is critical with a flat-tappet lifter, a race cam, and the strong racing valvesprings that must be used to keep the valvetrain under control. "Wiping" a cam lobe, or knocking the crown off the nose of the cam, is all too common if the engine isn't broken in gently and will show up as excessive valve lash.

A lifter failure is the second way lash can open up, and it is most common with roller lifters. This happens when the axle for the roller breaks or the needle bearings supporting the roller get crushed. This allows the lifter to sink lower in the lifter bore and open up the lash. When this happens, the lifter is very likely to damage the camshaft, so both will probably have to be replaced. Of course, that's still better than having to replace an entire engine because chunks of lifter were ground up inside the engine.

Check the Timing

If you notice that your engine won't hold its ignition timing consistently, it is probably the result of a stretched timing chain.

Engine ignition timing should be checked before every race. This is not only to ensure you have maximum power when you hit the track, but it is also a good insurance policy. If, for some reason, the distributor has been moved while the car was in the shop and the ignition timing is advanced too far, it can lead to damaging detonation under racing conditions.

It is also important to keep a regular check on your engine's timing to make sure the distributor and entire ignition system are working correctly. A worn timing chain can also throw your ignition timing off and will need to be replaced.

Check the Oil Filter

If your engine utilizes a dry-sump oiling system, it is relatively easy to pull the Oberg filter, which is a fine-mesh wire screen placed over the inlet to the oil reservoir, and inspect it for engine debris.

Although it is a little more involved with a wet-sump engine, checking for debris in the oil should still be done. The easiest method for this is to simply cut the oil filter canister open and check for debris in the filter element. Many companies, like Powerhouse Products, sell oil filter cutters designed specifically for this purpose. The idea is to cut the metal canister of the filter open so you can remove the filter element and inspect

If you notice that your engine won't hold its ignition timing consistently, it is probably the result of a stretched timing chain.

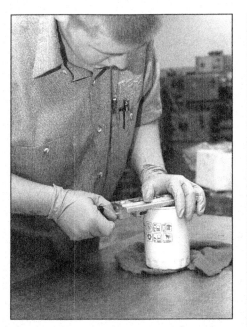

Don't try to cut apart a metal canister oil filter with a pair of tin snips or a cutoff wheel. It's too messy and will likely end with you bleeding. Instead, there are several models of oil filter cutters available that will open up a filter cleanly and easily to allow you to check the filter media for engine debris.

Every time you lash the valves, take an extra moment to check the spring pressures in at least four locations randomly. A valvespring will almost always lose pressure before it breaks, and this is a good way to catch a failing spring before it can cause catastrophic damage to your engine.

it.

With a new engine you will probably see small flecks of silicone and some aluminum from the pistons. There may be a few small pieces of steel, but if there are large pieces or there continue to be flecks of steel in the filter element after several runs you might have a problem.

The most likely source of steel filings in your filter element is the bearings flaking, but it can also be from just about anywhere else in the engine. If you cannot tell steel from aluminum by sight, you can use a small magnet to separate the materials. The steel will be attracted to the magnet while the aluminum will not.

When your engine is new, try to check your filter after break-in and again after your first race or two. If

you have no concerns after that, there is no need to destroy an oil filter every week. You can back off and only check your filter media after an oil change.

Check the Valvesprings

Given enough time and abuse, your valvesprings are guaranteed to fail eventually, no matter how much you spent on them. Catching a valvespring that's going bad before it actually fails can be the difference in replacing a $10 spring and going through a complete rebuild with a bent valve, a broken piston, a damaged cylinder head, and who knows what else.

The best way to monitor the health of your valvesprings is to track the spring pressures from the

You can spend several hundred dollars on a high-end on-head spring-pressure tester, but it isn't necessary. Moroso makes one that works on a simple spring design and is available from most catalogs, like Summit Racing, for around $75. It may not be as accurate as the more expensive models, but it is consistent, and that's the only thing that matters when you are checking for failing valvesprings.

moment you put the engine together and every week you race. All you need is an on-head spring checker—Moroso sells one for around $75—a notepad, and an ink pen. Begin by checking all your spring pressures when the springs are brand new. Don't depend on the rating on the box; check them yourself mounted on the cylinder head with the spring checker you will use week after week. It doesn't matter what reading the checker gives you as long as it is consistent and you use that same tool every time you check your springs.

Typically, a valvespring will show a drop-off in spring pressure during break-in. It is usually five percent of the spring's total pressure or less. After that it will take a set, and the pressure will remain steady at this plateau. When a spring, or springs, starts to lose pressure again, that's a sign that it is about to fail. You should pull any springs exhibiting signs of failure immediately rather than risk a spring breaking while you are on the racetrack.

Set up a system to check at least four valvesprings randomly every time you lash the valves. This is the easiest time since you will already have the valve covers off anyway. Write your findings in your logbook. This makes it easy to see if a spring, or springs, is losing pressure since the last check. Vigilant use of this method can virtually eliminate spring failures.

Teardown and Rebuild

There is a lot you can learn at the teardown stage. This is the time to detect problems before they become failures, monitor trends in wear, and know what you need for the rebuild so you won't be scrambling for parts

Dorton says that the engine should receive a complete visual inspection before removing the first bolt. This is a good time to check all the plug wires for burns or other damage. Because Dorton knows this engine was run hot, he will pay extra attention to areas most susceptible to heat, including gaskets and the oil pump, which can be checked visually. The heads and block are also susceptible to damage from overheating and will be Magnafluxed.

on Friday night. The focus definitely should be on spotting potential problems before they happen, but the procedures outlined here can also help you discover ways to improve engine performance, minimize engine downtime, and reduce the possibility that mistakes find their way into the engine at the rebuild stage.

I followed Keith Dorton as he tore down and inspected a Chevrolet engine that recently came into his shop. The owner sent it in early for a rebuild because it ran hot in its third race. Both the owner and Dorton suspect the problem is in the cooling system, but they want to make sure the engine hasn't suffered

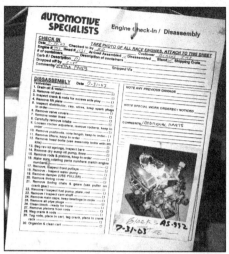

Dorton uses a standardized teardown sheet that makes sure no critical steps are missed. Parts that must be replaced are also listed here so that when it comes time for the build, everything is ordered and ready. Finally, Dorton includes a photo of the engine that he can quickly reference to see how all the brackets and accessories were originally installed.

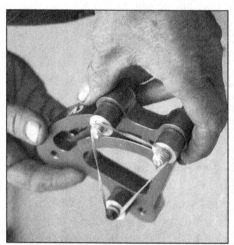

Some of the first items to come off the engine are all of the brackets. This power-steering bracket is a good example, as most have unique bolt sizes and spacers of different lengths. You can use a simple rubber band strung around the bolts to keep them and all the spacers in the right places. This can save a lot of headaches during re-assembly.

When pulling the rocker arms, ensure that no rocker bolt is ever loosened when under tension from the camshaft. This could bend the shaft slightly from the force of the valvespring. Instead, turn the engine over as you go so that the corresponding lifter for the rocker you are working on is on the base circle of the cam.

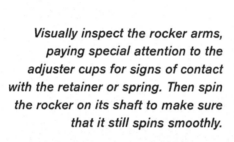

Visually inspect the rocker arms, paying special attention to the adjuster cups for signs of contact with the retainer or spring. Then spin the rocker on its shaft to make sure that it still spins smoothly.

An area of weakness in Chevrolet heads is the area between the two inside exhaust valves. You can see the discoloration the heat has caused on this head, but it isn't enough for concern.

Because he knows this engine has run hot, Dorton is on the lookout for signs of heat damage. One interesting tip is that the head bolts on a heat-damaged engine are often easy to remove. The heat allows the bolt holes to open up and the bolts to lose their stretch. Dorton says if you can remove the head bolts with a speed wrench, it's a sure sign the engine has been run hot.

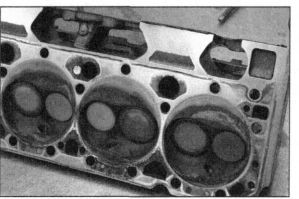

An important part of an engine builder's job is to look for trends. Dorton is careful to note the location of each spark plug at teardown and hang on to them. If he sees something that concerns him later on, he still has the plugs he can go back to and check.

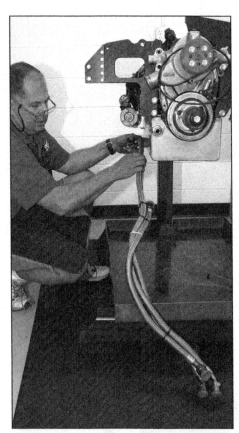

If you plan to reuse your hoses, make sure to plug them immediately as they are removed from the engine. They still need to be cleaned and checked, but this is your best defense against foreign materials infiltrating the system. Also, if you are using insulators, check to make sure they aren't camouflaging a collapsed hose.

Next to come out are the pistons and rods. Inspect underneath the piston crowns for discoloration from heat, the skirts for scuffing, and around the pin bosses for cracks.

An early sign of a failing oil pump is a rough feeling as you turn the pulley.

Most racing classes mandate flat-top pistons, and the weakest point for these pistons is normally between the two valve pockets. This piston is an extreme example, but if you intend to reuse your pistons in a rebuild, make sure to check here for cracks.

The damper is held onto the crank by an interference fit. Like the head bolts, if it comes off too easily once the crank bolt is removed, there's a problem.

You've probably already checked the Oberg or canister oil filter for metal, but it is also a good idea to give the inside of the oil pan a good inspection. You probably will need to remove the windage tray to be able to see in all the nooks and crannies, but it will have to come off for cleaning anyway.

One pin wouldn't drop straight out when the ring locks were removed. This can be a sign that the cylinder has suffered from detonation and the pin bore has been hammered. These pistons will be replaced anyway, but it is just one more clue to what is going on inside the engine.

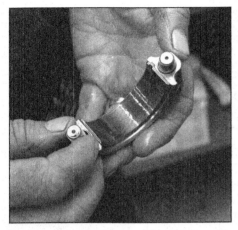

If you are just doing a refresh, you will want to reuse your bearings if possible. If they don't snap in and hold tight to the rods, they need to be replaced.

The crank should always be Magnafluxed on a rebuild. If there is a crack it will most often be in the snout area.

Magnafluxing the cam will reveal any cracks, but also check the lobes to make sure the crowns haven't been worn down, which is especially critical on flat-tappet cams. Also check the teeth on the timing gears on both the cam and distributor for damage or excessive wear.

The spider web that has formed on the top of this main bearing is a sign of excess heat.

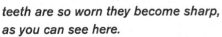

The distributor gear should be considered a sacrificial part because it is designed to wear, saving the much more expensive cam. A distributor gear should be replaced when the teeth are so worn they become sharp, as you can see here.

When removing bearings, never push them out sideways. If you do, it is possible to raise a burr on the tang. Then, the next time they are installed they will not seat properly. Even a difference as small as a couple thousandths of an inch can be a problem.

Pull the heads apart so you can check the status of the valve seats and valveguides.

Even though the valves and springs will be replaced for this rebuild, Dorton still checks the spring pressures so he can get an idea of how they are holding up over a number of races.

Pro Tip: Get Organized

You don't have to be running an engine shop or producing several race engines a week to benefit from some organizational tools. These can be especially helpful during teardown because they can help you keep each component organized with the cylinder it goes with.

For example, once a flat-tappet lifter breaks in with a cam lobe, it must always be mated to that lobe. On a rebuild you must make sure that it goes back into the same lifter bore that it came out of. A good valvetrain organizer tray can help eliminate mix-ups where the wrong lifter goes in the wrong spot. It can also help keep you from losing parts and keeps them clean until the engine is ready for reassembly.

Valve-train components are among the most stressed in a race engine, so it is important to handle them carefully. Even letting them "clink" together can cause stress risers. You can use valvetrain organizer trays that not only protect the parts but also keep them in order as they were removed from the engine.

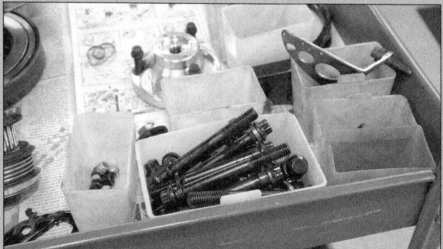

Speaking of racks for organization, here's another good tip. Use small plastic containers—lots of 'em—to keep all of your nuts, bolts, and other odds and ends separated.

ENGINE BUILD SHEET

Customer _____ Engine # _____ Date: _____

Engine Type _____ New/Rebuild _____

Comments _____

_____

Bore _____ Stroke _____ C.I./CYL. _____

Heads _____ Rings _____ Piston _____

Crank _____ Rod _____ Rod Length _____

Pin Type _____ Size _____ Deck _____

Dome Vol/Gasket _____ C.R. _____

Block Height _____ Comments _____

Cam _____ Serial # _____

Lifter _____ Other _____

	Opening		Closing					DUR @ .020	DUR @ .050
	0.020	0.050	0.020	0.050	TDC				
IN							IN		
EX							EX		

Lobe Separation _____ Center Line   IN _____ EX _____

IN Lobe Lift _____ EX. Lobe Lift _____

IN Lobe @ 10 ATDC _____ EX. Lobe @10 BTDC _____

Crank Key _____ Comments _____

Piston/Valve Intake _____ Valve Pocket Cut _____

Piston/Valve Exhaust _____ Valve Pocket Cut _____

Final Piston/Valve Intake _____ Exhaust _____

IN Rocker Ratio _____ EX Rocker Ratio _____

Gross Lift @ Valve   IN _____ EX _____

Mains	1	2	3	4	5
Crank					
Clearance					
Bearing Size					

Heads _____ Head # _____ CC _____

Push Rods _____ Length: IN _____ EX _____ Wall _____

Comments _____

_____

Signature _____

SOURCE GUIDE

Automotive Specialists
4357 Triple Crown Dr.
Concord, NC 28027
704/786-0187
www.automotivespecialists.com

Clements Racing Engines
6011 Melvin Drive
Spartanburg, SC 29303
864/576-0141
www.houseofpower.com

KT Engine Development
384 Industrial Ct.
Concord, NC 28025
704/784-2610

Manufacturers List

Automotive Racing Products
(ARP)
1863 Eastman Ave
Ventura, CA 93003
800/826-3045
www.arp-bolts.com

Carrillo Industries
990 Calle Amanecer
San Clemente, CA 92673
949/498-1800
www.carriloind.com

Clevite
1350 Eisenhower Pl.
Ann Arbor, MI 48108
800/248-9606
www.engineparts.com

Cloyes
6101 Phoenix Ave. #2
Ft. Smith, AR 72903
479/963-2105
www.cloyes.com

Comp Cams
3406 Democrat Rd.
Memphis, TN 38118
800/999-0853
www.compcams.com

Craftsman
Visit your local Sears store
www.craftsman.com

Crane
530 Fentress Boulevard
Daytona Beach, FL 32114
386/258-6167
www.cranecams.com

Crower Cams and Equipment
6180 Business Center Court
San Diego, CA 92154
619/661-6477
www.crower.com

CV PRoducts
42 High Tech Blvd.
Thomasville, NC 27360
800/448-1223
www.cvproducts.com

Dan Olson Racing Products
2744 North Argyle
Fresno, CA 93727
559/292-7267
www.olsonmotorsports.com

Dart Machinery
353 Oliver Street
Troy, MI 48084
248/362-1188
www.dartheads.com

Dyer's Top Rods
P.O. Box 596
619 N. Center St.
Forrest, IL 61741
800/867-7637
www.dyersrods.com

Edelbrock
2700 California St.
Torrance, CA 90503
800/416-8628
www.edelbrock.com

Federal Mogul
26555 Northwestern Highway
Southfield, Michigan 48033
248/354-7700
www.federal-mogul.com

Fel Pro
26555 Northwestern Highway
Southfield, Michigan 48033
248/354-7700
www.federal-mogul.com

Gear Wrench
14600 York Rd.; Suite A
Sparks, MD 21152
800/688-8939
www.gearwrench.com

General Motors Performance
Parts (GMPP)
See your local GM dealer
www.gmperformanceparts.com

Goodson Shop Supplies
P.O. Box 847
Winona, MN 55987-0847
800/533-8010
www.goodson.com

Holley
1801 Russellville Rd.
Bowling Green, KY 42101
270/781-9741
www.holley.com

Howards Cams
280 West 35th Ave.
Oshkosh, WI 54902
920/233-5228
www.howardscams.com

Ingersoll Rand
P.O. Box 970
1467 Rt. 31 South
Annandale, NJ 08801
800/866-5457
www.irtools.com

JE Pistons
15312 Connector Lane
Huntington Beach, CA 92649
714/898-9764
www.jepistons.com

Jesel
1985 Cedar Bridge Ave.
Lakewood, NJ 08701
732/901-1800
www.jesel.com

K1 Technologies
889 76th Street, Unit 6
Byron Center, MI 49315
616/583-9700
www.k1technologies.com

Mahle Motorsports
270 Rutledge Rd.
Fletcher, NC 28732
828/650-0802
www.us.mahle.com

Meta-Lax
Bonal Technologies
1300 North Campbell Rd.
Royal Oak, MI 48067
248/582-0900
www.meta-lax.com

Moroso
80 Carter Drive
Guilford, CT 06437-2116
203/458-0542
www.moroso.com

Performance Distributors
2699 Barris Drive
Memphis, TN 38132
901/396-5782
www.performance
distributors.com

Powerhouse Products
3402 Democrat Rd.
Memphis, TN 38118
800/872-7223
www.powerhouseproducts.co

Royal Purple
One Royal Purple Lane
Porter, TX 77365
281/354-8600
www.royalpurple.com

Shaver Wesmar
Wesmar Racing Engines
14502 South Lewis
Bixby, OK 74008
918/366-7311
www.wesmarracing.com

Speed Pro
26555 Northwestern Highway
Southfield, Michigan 48033
248/354-7700
www.federal-mogul.com

Summit Racing
P.O. Box 909
Akron, OH 44398-6177
330/630-0240
www.summitracing.com

T&D Machine Products
4859 Convair Dr.
Carson City, NV 89706
775/884-2292
www.tdmach.com

Wiseco
7201 Industrial Park Blvd.
Mentor, OH 44060-5396
800/321-1364
www.wiseco.com

World Products
51 Trade Zone Court
Ronkonkoma, NY 11779
631/981-1918
www.worldcastings.com

CPSIA information can be obtained
at www.ICGtesting.com
Printed in the USA
BVOW04s0841271217

502998BV00041B/672/P

9 781613 250099